The Best of Everything at the Jersey Shore

The Best of Everything at the Jersey Shore

BY JEFF EDELSTEIN

New Jersey Monthly Press

Morristown, New Jersey

Library of Congress Catalog Card Number 99-70643

The Best of Everything at the Jersey Shore

10 INTRODUCTION

13 CHAPTER I
THE TOWNS

15 Five Towns for You, Me, the Kids,
Your Cousin Larry, and the Babysitter

21 Three Towns That the Brady
Bunch Would Feel Comfortable In

24 Six Towns That Treat Relaxation
As If It Were a Tiki Goddess

29 Two Towns That Wear Their
History on Their Bathing Trunks

31 Two Towns That Stay Up Late
Enough for Last Call

33 Two Towns That
Aren't Even Towns

35 Twelve Towns and Beaches That Don't Fit
Any Category but Are Too Much a Part
of Shore Lore to Leave Out

41 CHAPTER II
BEYOND THE BEACH

42 Boardwalks and Other
Beach Amusements

45 Gone Fishin'

46 Won't You Let Me
Take You on a Sea Cruise?

48 Whoop-Whoop-Whoa-
Zow-Eeeeee-Yikes

49 Tame and Dry

50 Mom! I'm Bored!!
I Said I'm Bored!!!

52 Shore History 101

54 It's Time for
Some Culture

55 Natural Wonders

57 Nine Types of Seashells You
Might Find at the Shore

57 Shop 'Til You Drop,
Then Crawl

SANDY HOOK
SEA BRIGHT
LONG BRANCH
DEAL
ASBURY PARK
OCEAN GROVE
BRADLEY BEACH
AVON
BELMAR
SPRING LAKE
SEA GIRT
MANASQUAN
POINT PLEASANT BEACH
BAY HEAD
MANTOLOKING
LAVALLETTE
SEASIDE HEIGHTS
SEASIDE PARK
ISLAND BEACH
BARNEGAT LIGHT
LOVELADIES
SURF CITY
SHIP BOTTOM
BRANT BEACH
BEACH HAVEN
BRIGANTINE
ATLANTIC CITY
VENTNOR
MARGATE
LONGPORT
OCEAN CITY
SEA ISLE CITY
AVALON
STONE HARBOR
THE WILDWOODS
CAPE MAY
CAPE MAY POINT

63 CHAPTER III
EAT, DRINK, AND BE MERRY

64 Start the Day Right:
Best Breakfasts

66 Seafood, and
Only Seafood

68 Ice Cream

70 Pizza

71 Lunch

73 Stuff You Know You Shouldn't Eat,
But You Can't Help Yourself

75 Dinner for Two (or Four, or Six, or Eight,
or Everyone You Appreciate)

78 Bars and Clubs and
Drinking and Dancing

83 CHAPTER IV
ATLANTIC CITY

84 A Little
History

85 Things
to Do

86 Six Popular
Casino Games

88 The Hotels

93 CHAPTER V
EVERYTHING ELSE UNDER THE SUN

94 Getting There

95 Finding a Place to Stay

97 Ten Great Cape May Bed-and-Breakfasts/
Guest Houses

100 Ten Souvenirs You Must
Come Home With

105 Photography Credits

107 Index

Welcome.

Sit down, get comfy. In fact, take the phone off the hook. You won't want to be bothered. If you want any refreshments, I suggest you get them now. We've got a lot of ground to cover, or at least the ground from Sandy

Hook to Cape May. 🐚 The New Jersey Shore is one of the greatest beaches in the world. So say I, who spent the better part of the summer of 1998 traversing it. The coastline is almost completely uninterrupted over the course of its 127 miles, and despite nature's battering, the overwhelming majority of the sand remains. And it's not just the sand and surf that makes the Jersey Shore what it is. I'm talking about the boardwalks, the restaurants, the people, and Lucy the Elephant. Do you know Lucy? If you don't, you will soon. 🐚 Although it's a cliche to say so, there is indeed something for everyone at the Jersey Shore. I hope that I can help with your soon-to-be-had experiences. 🐚 This book is broken down into four distinct sections, and a not-so-distinct fifth. The first section deals specifically with the towns: who goes there, what you can find there, and why you may or may not want to visit there. The second section delves into the "things-to-do" aspect of shore life, from amusement parks to historical attractions. The third section takes you on a whirlwind culinary tour of the Shore. The fourth section takes you on an equally whirlwind tour of Atlantic City. And the fifth deals with subjects not covered in the previous sections. 🌀 I know what you're thinking: This does not make for a linear book. Well, you're right. It's not. Well, not exactly. Each

of the first three sections goes from north to south, so you won't need to check your compass while you read the book. Within those geographical guidelines, I'll be taking you from town to town, from pizza joint to jazz club, from surf to sand, and back again. This is a

selective guide; there's so much to see and do at the Shore that reading a book that tried to tell you everything about every place would take up all your time, and you'd never get around to the trip itself. What you'll find here is a blend of highlights and all-time favorites, punctuated by some personal picks of my own. 🌀 The book is aimed at those of you who plan to vacation during the summer months. Parts of the Jersey Shore, most notably towns like Ocean Grove and Cape May, stay open year-round. In some other towns, many of the restaurants are open year-round, but there aren't many other off-season activities. If you plan to use this book during the nonsummer months, please call ahead to any place you might want to stop at. As a matter of fact, to avoid disappointment, it's always a good idea to call ahead before a visit—winter, spring, summer, or fall. 🌀 Are you still comfy? Is the phone still off the hook? Good. Enjoy the book, but more important, enjoy the beach. I know I will.

CHAPTER I

THE TOWNS

It's been said by many a Chamber of Commerce that *its* town offers up the best of everything. Well, that's their job. My job, however, is more difficult. What I will try to do here is tell you which towns offer up the best of...well, everything. Maybe the difference isn't so obvious.

Let's start over. Each town along the New Jersey Shore offers one constant: the beach. If all you want to do is grab a dog-eared paperback and slap yourself on a chair, then any Shore spot is as good as any other. If, however, you think you might actually like to take in the local flavors, then some towns are better than others. Perhaps you're looking for a bit of history. Well, the same rule applies. Or maybe it's roller coasters that tickle your fancy. Well, as my Aunt Matilda once said, there ain't no pop-a-wheelies in Ocean Grove. Or something to that effect.

Going to the Jersey Shore is more than just picking a place to go and getting there. If it were that easy, then I wouldn't be writing this book, would I? The fact is that each town has its own personality. Some are loud and rambunctious and hyperactive, while others are quiet and polite and not active at all, and still others exhibit both sides of that coin. Choosing a vacation spot is not, if you'll pardon the pun, a toss-up. In fact, I've done my best here to treat it as an exact science. I take my job seriously, folks.

So slather on some SPF 15, pop the Beach Boys in the CD player, and throw on those goofy sunglasses you bought in 1979. It's time to find out where you're going this summer.

Five Towns for You, Me, the Kids, Your Cousin Larry, and the Babysitter

These five towns all exhibit the classic Shore town motif of sun and fun for everyone: for families, for kids, for young adults, for the grandparents. It's hard to go wrong by checking in to any of these towns for a week or two.

Belmar

Belmar grows in the summer like a ripening peach. Families come for the relatively inexpensive accommodations, and those ever-present Generation X'ers come for the same reason. And they're the ones who run the show. Not that a family can't enjoy a great time, but you should be ready to deal with any of the following: beer cans strewn about, loud music piercing the night air, tires squealing, and rambunctious post-midnight shouts of "Whoo-hoo." With a handful of great nightspots in town, Belmar is destination number one for weekend partyers and summer rental groups of fifteen or more. Not that most Belmar rental homes are mansions. In fact, the majority are certainly on the smallish side, but close quarters aren't exactly a problem with the younger set. If you're not renting a house, other options in Belmar include staying at one of the hotels or guest houses in town or coming to Belmar on a day trip.

A LITTLE HISTORY Belmar covers approximately one square mile of land and is surrounded by water on all sides: Shark River Inlet, Lake Como, and the Atlantic do the combined trick. Believe it or not, surfers were not the first people to settle the land; that honor went to the Leni Lenape Nation, followed by groups of European farmers. In 1872, a group of businessmen purchased the land, and by 1890 Belmar, then known as the Ocean Beach Association, was a major resort area. Today you can take a self-guided walking tour through Belmar and inspect for yourself the houses and buildings that were built way back when. Call the Belmar Municipal Office Tourism Information Line (732-681-3700, ext. 2) for details.

THINGS TO DO THE SIMPLEST THING FOR ME TO DO IS TELL YOU TO CALL THE TOURISM HOTLINE (732-681-0005) OR CHECK OUT WWW.BELMAR.COM for the latest, but you'll find concerts at the Huisman Gazebo every Tuesday at 8 PM, social dancing at Taylor Pavilion

Keeping Busy in Belmar

CONCERTS AT HUISMAN GAZEBO AND PAYANOE PLAZA

DANCING AT TAYLOR PAVILION

VOLLEYBALL AT THE BEACH

BOATING AT THE BELMAR MARINA

STROLLING AT THE BOARDWALK

on Thursdays at 8 PM, and the Payanoe Plaza Concert Series on Fridays at 7 PM. And in late August, throw on you Adidas, because the annual Belmar Five Mile Run will take place with or without you. For boating enthusiasts, the Belmar Marina has long been the main home for many motorboats and sailboats in Monmouth County. You can rent outboard motorboats, kayaks, or rowboats there, hop aboard a party boat, or do a little fishing.

THE BEACH The beach at Belmar, known as the Miracle Mile, gets a decent mix of families and Gen-Xers, if only because for much of the day many of those Gen-Xers are still sleeping off the remnants of the previous evening. The Fourteenth Street beach is the hangout for the young and tragically hip, with surf shorts on the men and a lot of string bikinis on the women. The stretch from Eighteenth to Twentieth is definitely more family oriented, and the volleyball nets at Eighteenth Street are sure to draw crowds, especially every July when the professional tour rolls around. A boardwalk runs the length of the shoreline, but it has no games or rides–it's just a great place to walk or jog or relax the day away. Badges are available at the Taylor Pavilion on Fifth Avenue: rates are $5 daily, $40 for the season. For senior citizens (sixty-two and up), the rate falls to $10 a season, and children under fifteen go to the beach free.

Beach Haven

Beach Haven is a convenient trip from just about anywhere in New Jersey.

Beach Haven has, and this is a good thing, a dual personality. By day it's a lovely, mild-mannered beach town, a haven if you will. And even up to early evening, there is little change in the air. Parents and children can shower off the sand from a day at the beach, head out for some dinner at one of the many fine restaurants, and then, perhaps, get some ice cream for dessert. At this point, some families may head over to the Fantasy Island Amusement Park, and others may decide to check out the show at the Surflight Theater. At around 10 PM, however, things change noticeably. The teenagers are let loose, milling about town, and the over-twenty-one crowd has started to make its way from the rental homes to the many bars in town.

Not that families and singles don't manage to coexist. In fact, they do, quite nicely. Part of the reason is that, generally speaking, the singles set is a more subdued group than you might find at Seaside or Belmar. Another reason is geography. From most parts of New Jersey, Beach Haven is a not particularly feasible place to go just for the night, or just for the day, for that matter. Most people rent either for the week or for the entire summer. There are also numerous hotels and motels besides the rental homes.

THINGS TO DO Besides Fantasy Island Park and the Surflight Theater, Beach Haven offers free concerts at Veterans Bicentennial Park throughout the summer, as well as many other town-sponsored events. Your best bet would be to stop in at the Southern Ocean County Chamber of Commerce. You can't miss it—after you cross the bridge to the island, it will be on your left, a few blocks down. YOU CAN ALSO CALL THE CHAMBER AT 609-494-7211 BEFORE YOU PLAN YOUR VACATION TO SEE WHAT WILL BE HAPPENING WHILE YOU'RE THERE. Beach Haven is a great bicycling town, with bike lanes going in both directions. The only hazard to watch out for is the in-line skaters, who also use the lanes.

THE BEACHES Beach Haven has suffered recently from erosion, especially around Tenth Street. Nonetheless, they remain some of the most popular in the state, with families and twenty-somethings dotting the landscape. Known as the Queen City Six Miles at Sea, the town of Beach Haven is truly a star attraction for all types of beachgoers, including the surfers. Check out the beach at Holyoke Avenue, where some of the best waves at the Shore are found. Seasonal badges cost $12 if bought before June 15, $15 after. Weekly and daily rates are $7 and $3, respectively.

To many, Seaside Heights is the essence of the Jersey Shore.

Seaside Heights

What a name, what a town. Overrun by families and teenagers, Seaside Heights is what the Shore is all about. The beaches are wide, and the bathing suits aren't. There are plenty of motels in town, and there are also plenty of houses to rent. The town is inexpensive, and the thrill is always there. So what if there aren't any five-star restaurants—who needs 'em? Not anybody who decides to spend some time in Seaside Heights.

The big draw of Seaside Heights can certainly be found at the boardwalk. Although it's only a mile long, there is so much hubbub all around that you feel as if it goes on forever. The town itself, especially once the sun goes down, has the same feel. Everything is so bright, so packed together, that's it's hard to believe that such a small town can offer so much. We're not talking high culture here, not by a long shot. Seaside Heights is the place to go for fun. It's no wonder that MTV decided to broadcast from there in the summer of 1998. Where else could they have gone?

THINGS TO DO For nighttime entertainment, the boardwalk is the place to be for both the young and old. The two amusement piers boast some great rides, and there are some good bars right there on the boards. There aren't all that many town-sponsored events, but you can find about whatever's going on by calling the SEASONAL INFORMATION NUMBER: 732-793-1510.

THE BEACH The Seaside Heights beaches are as wide as any on the northern Shore. It's a good thing, too, because people flock to them in droves. There is a motley mix of families and seniors—that's both types of seniors, of course, the senior seniors and the last-year-of-high-school seniors. After all, many of the people who own houses in Seaside Heights have owned them for a good while and have decided to keep coming there even though the town is somewhat overrun with the young folk. Surprisingly, there rarely seems to be a generational problem in Seaside Heights. Everybody's having too much fun.

Beach badges are more than reasonable, with Wednesdays and Thursdays free, a charge of $2 on Mondays, Tuesdays, and Fridays, and $4 on Saturdays, Sundays, and holidays. For the season, the price is $35; kids under twelve go to the beach free. The beach at Casino Pier between Sherman and Grant Avenues is the place to go if you want to surf or fish.

The International Kite Festival is just one of the many summer activities held in Wildwood.

Wildwood

Wildwood is packed all summer long with mostly weekly guests who are there to sample the incredibly wide beaches and the incredibly long boardwalk. Finding a place to stay in Wildwood is never really a problem. There are 14,000 hotel and motel rooms to choose from, and the sheer number of options makes the prices oh-so-very-reasonable. If you want to know who goes there, a better question may be, Who doesn't go there? And the answer to that question is: anyone seeking a quiet time. From sunup to sundown, and then from sundown to 3 AM (when the bars close), there is something for everybody. If you're a family looking for fun, Wildwood has it. If you're a kid looking to break away from the family, Wildwood can accommodate you. If you want to go to a club, drink your face off, and dance until your limbs turn lame, Wildwood is certainly the place to hang out.

THINGS TO DO Special events dot the Wildwood calendar all summer long. The typical concerts and fireworks are always an attraction, but it's the different stuff that's such a hoot. For example, you have the National Marbles Tournament, the Mummer's Brigade Weekend, and on July 25, Santa Claus drops by North Wildwood Beach for a half-year check on who exactly has been naughty or nice. Other events you probably won't find anywhere else include the Polka Spree-by-the-Sea, the National Speed Slide Championships at Raging Waters, and the Model Aircraft Beach Fly-In. Some off-season events include the New Jersey State Harley Owner's Group Rally, the Boardwalk Classic Car Show, and the Irish Fall Festival, all held in September. May brings the International Kite Festival and Pirates Weekend, featuring a special guest appearance by the notorious Captain Kidd. FOR BOATLOADS OF INFOR-MATION, CALL 1-800-WW-BY-SEA OR POINT YOUR WEARY WEB BROWSER TO WWW.WILDWOODS.COM.

THE BEACH Wildwood's beach is New Jersey's greatest anomaly. While virtually every other beach in the state is losing sand the way most of my friends are losing their hair, Wildwood's sand deposits continue to grow luxuriously. It's like the Sahara out there. At some points, it's a half-mile walk from sand to surf. A friendly tip: Bring sandals, and perhaps a camel. Obviously, the size of the beach means that you'll probably be able to find a spot to call your own without having other people trampling on your towels. And as an added bonus, the price of admission is zero.

Wildwood's Great White Roller Coaster

Sea Isle City

Once principally the domain of the social security set, Sea Isle City has emerged in recent years as a family destination, as well as party central when the sun goes down. During the day, the town is similar to Ocean City. There are many two-family dwellings, and Mom and Dad and Sis and Bro can be found making their way to the beach. At night, there's no shortage of bars, and no shortage of people making the pilgrimage to them. The majority of vacationers choose to rent a home for a week, mostly because there are few motels and hotels to choose from.

Motels and guest houses are plentiful at the Shore, but book your space early—they fill up quickly for the summer season.

THINGS TO DO There are many things to do with the children, such as Play by the Bay, between Fifty-ninth and Sixty-third Streets at Central Avenue, an all-wooden playground that was built and paid for by the community. It also has basketball and tennis courts. If you're in the mood for boardwalk-style attractions, check out Fun City, described best by Michael Callahan, former senior editor at *New Jersey Monthly*, when he said that it's something like a church carnival plopped in the school parking lot. Other attractions that make Sea Isle City perfect for the youngsters are such activities as the Beachcomber Walks, held at the Twenty-ninth Street Beach on Tuesdays and Thursdays. These are guided tours that take you along the beach, and you learn about the shells, the birds, the ocean—anything that has to do with the beach. The tour is indeed both fun and educational.

In the evening, however, the educational part of Sea Isle City gets tossed like so many beer cans, and it becomes a party town. Smack in the middle of the city are such tried-and-true nightspots as the Springfield Inn. The over-twenty-ones flock to Sea Isle City much as they do in Belmar and Seaside.

If you're not in the mood for pouring shots down your throat and walking around in puddles of Budweiser, then another way to spend your evenings in Sea Isle City is at free Concerts Under the Stars, which take place at the Promenade and JFK Boulevard on Monday and Wednesday nights. From classical strings to Dixieland bands, chances are you'll find something to your liking. FOR MORE INFORMATION, CALL THE SEA ISLE CITY TOURISM COMMISSION AT 609-263-TOUR.

THE BEACHES The good folks of Sea Isle City pride themselves on the fine quality of their beach. Virtually all South Jersey Shore towns had to rebuild at least parts of their beaches after storms in the early 1990s, and it's clear that Sea Isle City did some of the best work. The northern beaches are somewhat quieter than the southern ones, but all the beaches are pristine: clean and generally perfect. There is no boardwalk, but there is a mile-and-a-half blacktop promenade, and that suits the in-line skaters just fine. Beaches are free on Wednesdays, and the prices otherwise are $13 for the season, $7 for the week, and $2 daily.

Three Towns That the Brady Bunch Would Feel Comfortable In

If you'd like to stay away from the rowdies, these towns offer the tops in family entertainment.

Point Pleasant Beach

Point Pleasant Beach has lots of shops and restaurants and is fun to walk around in. It has also done a wonderful job of holding on to its family atmosphere, mostly due to the Jenkinson family. You can visit Jenkinson's Aquarium, Jenkinson's Beach, Jenkinson's Amusements. Point Pleasant Beach retains the charm of an old-time Shore town, with mom-and-pop stores all over the place. You won't find many chain stores in town; almost everything is privately owned. As a result, the local population is among the friendliest along all of the Jersey Shore. The motels and guest houses are somewhat plentiful considering the size of the town, but fill up quickly for the summer.

THINGS TO DO At Jenkinson's Beach, every Monday at 7 PM brings the Kiddie Beach Show, featuring everything from magic to ponies, depending on the week. And every Tuesday there are Kiddie Concerts on the beach. Bring your Fisher-Price camera! Fireworks dot the summer sky on Thursdays at 9 PM on the boardwalk. Sundays, also at 9, feature a laser-light show at Jenkinson's Beach, and Wednesdays at 7:30 PM feature orchestral concerts at Jenkinson's Inlet Beach. On or around July 4, the Classic Car Cruise heads through the downtown area; leave your Taurus in the garage. August always brings the Giant Sand Castle Building Contest.

While Point Pleasant Beach is certainly no Ocean City when it comes to weird goings-on, it does offer its share of novelties. The summer of 1998, for instance, brought Penguin Appreciation Day at the Aquarium as well as Elvis Day on the boardwalk. You could ride the rides with the King, or at least with a reasonable facsimile. And if you came dressed as Elvis, whether the 1950s hipster or the 1970s crooner—wide hips, spangly jumpsuit, and all, you could get into the Aquarium or the Fun House for free. FOR DETAILS ABOUT ALL SUMMER EVENTS, AND ELVIS SIGHTINGS, CALL THE POINT PLEASANT CHAMBER OF COMMERCE AT 732-899-2424.

Point Pleasant Beach arcade

THE BEACH Well, of course, the main mile of beach that everybody uses is Jenkinson's, which runs north from Trenton Avenue. The other beach, Risden's, runs from Trenton Avenue south. Risden's is definitely the quieter of the two. Badges cost $4.50 daily, $5.50 on weekends, $1 for children ages five to eleven, and those little surfer dudes and dudettes under five are free. Seasonal badges are $60 for adults, $40 for the five-to-elevens, and free for the under-five set. The beach attracts everyone, locals and tourists alike, and is, of course, jam-packed on weekends. The family atmosphere definitely pervades the place during the week. The weekends see more of an influx of younger people, mostly there for the volleyball and the music, drink, and dance at Jenkinson's Pavilion Restaurant and Bar.

Surf City

Surf City is one of the prime family vacation towns around. Despite the presence of some pretty good bars, it's still a place for families to enjoy a groovy beach and great restaurants, and to have a swell time all around. There are few hotels in Surf City, and the majority of vacationers are there either for the summer or the week, renting houses.

THINGS TO DO Much like Beach Haven, Surf City is a great place to enjoy bicycling, in-line skating, and virtually any other activity that combines wheels with self-propulsion. For a less strenuous activity, head over to the bay side and go crabbing. You can rent the traps at any bait shop. There's the typical array of mini-golf courses, and there are also two playgrounds. FOR MORE INFORMATION, CALL THE SOUTHERN OCEAN COUNTY CHAMBER OF COMMERCE AT 609-494-7211.

THE BEACH Extending from North Twenty-fifth Street to South Third Street on Long Beach Island, Surf City's beaches are primarily for families. Surf City is also really the only town on the island that attracts day trippers. The beach is cordoned off from Twenty-third to Twenty-fifth Streets for fishing. For surfers, the best place is Twenty-fifth Street, but after 5 PM, you're only allowed to hang ten from First to Third Streets. Badges run $21 seasonally ($16 if purchased before May 31) and $5 daily. If you fall into the magical under twelve or over sixty-five categories, the beaches are yours for free.

Ocean City

Billing itself as America's greatest family resort, Ocean City prides itself on creating a fun and safe atmosphere for its visitors. It succeeds mightily. In fact, it's safe to say that it is New Jersey's greatest family resort. One reason that this is so is that Ocean City is a dry town, but the lack of liquor is not the main reason Ocean City is what it is. Which means that you can rightly assume that there are no drunkards milling about, which in turn leads to precious few boom boxes spewing forth gangsta rap, and so on and so forth. Ocean City is so special because it's downright fun, whether you're staying in a rented house or in one of the resort's many hotels, motels, or inns.

A LITTLE HISTORY Ocean City, much like Ocean Grove, was founded with the goal of building a lovely surfside community where the religious could relax while they prayed. Incredibly, the basic premise still holds. Substitute "family" for "religious," and substitute "pray to the sun god" for "pray," and there you have it. One of Ocean City's great claims to fame is that Grace Kelly spent summers there as a youngster. It probably hasn't changed much since that time; in fact, Ocean City still has an old-time feel to it—not in the architecture, certainly not in the prices, but in the generalities of the whole place. People are surprisingly nice in Ocean City.

THINGS TO DO The town sponsors literally hundreds of summertime events, from concerts at the Music Pier to the famous Weird Contest Week, held every August. One of the more interesting events held that week is the Miss Miscellaneous contest. The winner in the summer of 1998 paraded around in a Carmen Miranda getup, dancing the macarena and all the while twisting a hula hoop around her waist. Extraordinary talents, if you ask me. CALL 609-525-9300 FOR INFORMATION.

Ocean City also boasts a topflight boardwalk, featuring Gillian's Wonderland Pier at Sixth Street. Gillian's is definitely geared for the preteen-and-under set, as is much of the fun activity in Ocean City. Ocean City is not really a place for pouting teenagers, who abound on the Wildwood and Seaside boardwalks. Ocean City's boardwalk is the kind that simply calls out to be used in a Disney movie-of-the-week starring cute twins as sisters or best friends who conveniently lose their parents for a weekend and get into all sorts of silly trouble.

Family Fun in Ocean City

GILLIAN'S WONDERLAND PIER

THE MUSIC PIER

MARKET DAYS

THIRTY-FOURTH STREET BEACH

THE BEACH The beach in Ocean City is eight miles long, and every part of it is pristine. Despite being consistently hammered by storm after storm, somehow every summer the beach still looks as good as it did the summer before. Which part of the beach is the best? The Thirty-fourth Street beach is the best family beach in Ocean City. Sure, all the beaches in Ocean City are for families, but the Thirty-fourth Street beach stands out from the crowd, mostly for its proximity to food and restrooms, two of the most important requirements for a pleasant afternoon in the sun. Beach badges here are ridiculously inexpensive, as they are along much of the southern Jersey Shore. In 1998, the adult rates were $16 for the season, $6 for the week, and $3 for the day.

Don't leave Ocean City without sampling some Johnson's popcorn on the boardwalk. You'll want to take some home.

𝕡 𝕡 𝕡

Six Towns That Treat Relaxation As If It Were a Tiki Goddess

Bradley Beach

Bradley Beach is on the comeback trail. There are many new stores and restaurants along Main Street, and the summer tourist trade has picked up in recent years. The town has a decidedly 1950s feel to it, and you half expect Fonzie to come screeching around a corner on his motorcycle. Bradley Beach is definitely for the family seeking a low-key summer spot—there are no boardwalks or amusement park rides. People who go to Bradley Beach have probably been going there for years, either owning their own home, renting a house, or visiting their grandparents. It looks more like a regular town than a seashore spot.

THINGS TO DO What the town lacks in typical seaside ambience it more than makes up for with activities like musical programs held at the Victorian Gazebo between Brinley and Fifth Avenues. The summer of 1998, for instance, saw country-and-western music and dance instruction with Double D Productions. Wednesday nights brought Then & Now, with music from the 1950s and 1960s, and Thursday nights featured the Summer Youth Dances. Bradley Beach really seems to be partially stuck in the 1950s, and that is a good thing. FOR INFORMATION ABOUT OTHER SUMMER EVENTS, CALL THE RECREATION HOTLINE AT 732-776-2998.

THE BEACH There are lots of beaches in Bradley Beach, separated from each other by jetties. Every summer, one of the beaches is reserved for surfing, and that's as good an idea as I've ever heard. The prices for admission are $5.50 daily and $50 seasonally, and if you're over sixty or under fourteen, a seasonal badge can be yours for $25. The Ocean Avenue Beach is the place for families, with a playground and a mini-golf course right off the beach. The mini-golf course, for reasons beyond my understanding, is known as the Bradley Beach Golf Club.

Bay Head

The lovely hamlet of Bay Head is a delightful spot to spend a day, a weekend, a week, or, if you're Gatsby enough, a whole summer. Bay Head seems as if it belongs more along the New England coast than on our own. It's small, quiet, and towny. The majority of vacationers who frequent Bay Head have a place to call their own for the summer, whether they own their home or rent it. Many of the people who summer here are either senior citizens or families with young children, although there is also a large contingent of young, single, urban professional types who choose Bay Head over the Hamptons. The handful of bed-and-breakfasts and hotels in town attract the young, attached, urban professional type.

One thing to keep in mind about Bay Head is its rather prohibitive prices. Renting a house here is no $500-a-week deal. Most of the rentals go by the month, and we're talking prices that easily climb into the five figures. Gatsby enough, indeed. The B and Bs and hotels are no bargain either, with prices that start in the mid-hundreds for a weekend stay.

THINGS TO DO There is precious little to do here. Forget about amusement parks and rides and the like. Actually, the only real thing to do in Bay Head, besides going to the beach, is to take a stroll through its quaint shopping district. Or you could try to stow away on a fabulous yacht at the Bay Head Yacht Club.

THE BEACHES Not very long ago, the beach at Bay Head was open only to residents. The state sued the town, the state won, and now anyone can enjoy the beach at Bay Head. It's rarely crowded, so it's a great place to spend the day. A daily badge will run you $4.50, and a seasonal badge costs $50, but they must be bought in pairs; you can't buy a ticket without a partner or friend.

Spring Lake

Spring Lake is where many a moneyed family spends its summer at the Shore. The vast majority of vacationers own their homes, yet many of the stately older houses have been converted in recent years to bed-and-breakfasts. One of the grand aspects of Spring Lake used to be the sheer number of huge homes and old hotels that were all over town. Now, only the homes remain. The famed Essex and Sussex Hotel, which (a) is no longer a hotel and (b) has been shut down for years, still stands as testament to the old Spring Lake. The hotel is monstrous in its dimensions, and it's not hard to imagine days gone by, with women flocking to the beach in daring bathing costumes and men in straw hats talking about Babe Ruth. Today the women are probably wearing everyday clothing much more revealing than those daring bathing costumes, and the men may be talking about Mark McGwire. But the old-time aura still remains, and you'll be pleasantly surprised by the easy pace Spring Lakers enjoy. It's common to see people happily spending their days sitting on the porches of their homes or their bed-and-breakfasts, sipping lemonade and watching the people walk by.

Watching the world go by from your front porch is just one of the pleasures of a visit to Spring Lake.

THINGS TO DO Relaxation is the operative word here. You can take a stroll through the downtown shopping area and stop by the lake (Spring Lake; get it?) and marvel at the ducks and swans enjoying their stay in New Jersey. The park surrounding the lake feels more like a country retreat than a beach diversion, with all kinds of trees and shrubbery and paths throughout. You can also tour the town, checking out the architecture. CALL THE CHAMBER OF COMMERCE AT 732-449-0577 FOR MAPS AND THE LIKE.

THE BEACH The beaches at Spring Lake have been hit by the erosion bug, of course, but remain some of the most pristine beaches along the Shore. The boardwalk is l-o-n-g, without arcades and all that. It's just a classic boardwalk, albeit one made out of recycled plastic bags and wood chips, or what I like to call space-age polymers, just because it sounds cool. Of course, "space-age polymerwalk" doesn't have that Shore ring to it, so the term "boardwalk" still applies. At any time during the day, you'll find joggers, walkers, and the like doing the exercise thing, and also regular people out for a midday stroll, ogling the beachside mansions. The price for admission to the sand and surf is $3 daily and $43 for the season, while those under eleven get on for free.

Lavallette

Quiet, unassuming Lavallette has fallen under the collective radar of us shorebirds, and it's a shame. The town is a pitch-perfect rendition of what a fun little Shore stop should look and feel like. The main thoroughfare in town is Route 35 North, which sounds like a hustling bustling road but in fact isn't; it's just your typical little road through Anytown, USA. The road is magnificently wide, however, which makes Lavallette an excellent bike-riding town. There are all sorts of shops, restaurants, ice cream places, and other diversions right on the main drag for your enjoyment. And if you still haven't found what you're looking for, chances are the Ben Franklin five-and-ten store will have it, including possibly the largest collection of sand-castle-building equipment this side of the Mississippi.

The pail and shovel collection at Lavallette's Ben Franklin five-and-ten is the stuff childhood dreams and memories are made of.

As far as housing goes, you can spend as much or as little as you want. There are a handful of motels, some gorgeous houses, and some smaller cottages. There are choices for everyone, and everyone goes there—a solid mix of young and old, family and single, surfer and stroller. Lavallette, while certainly not a ritzy getaway, makes up for that with an all-out unpretentiousness that pervades the town. And to think—such a great town, such a great name for a town, and yet no Shore band has named itself the Lavallettes. A mystery to me.

THINGS TO DO Many people who stay in Lavallette go there for its quiet, unassuming quality. If you feel the need to let loose, Seaside Heights is right down the road.

THE BEACH Lavallette is one of the few Shore towns to take full advantage of its bay front by utilizing it as a beach. It's a great place to take children. The regular beach is good and wide, with no threat of a wave crashing down on your blanket. The badge prices for adults are reasonable: In 1998 they cost $30 for the summer. There's a small boardwalk by the beach that's pleasant to stroll on while admiring the sea and rolling the name Lavallette over and over on your tongue.

Stone Harbor/Avalon

First, I want to apologize to the respective Chambers of Commerce of both towns. I know that Stone Harbor and Avalon are two completely separate towns, and I really have no right to splash them together as I'm doing here. But please, let me explain.

For starters, the towns lie right next to each other. In fact, if you didn't know better, you would assume that the whole stretch is one town. The main drag in each town is the same road under different names, and the numbered streets that intersect it do not start over when you cross the border.

As far as the who-goes-there-aspect, that, too, is seemingly the same: mostly upper-middle-class families. Avalon and Stone Harbor are not cheap. Both are like traditional towns in their sense of community. There are sports clinics and tennis lessons, soccer games, and the like. While I was there, I actually bought lemonade at a stand run by a pair of seven-year-olds on their corner. A very friendly, safe atmosphere prevails in both these towns.

Tennis, soccer, and lemonade stands are fixtures of the Sone Harbor/Avalon summer scene.

THINGS TO DO One chief difference between the two towns is that there are more restaurants and nightlife on the Avalon side, while the shopping is concentrated in Stone Harbor, especially at Ninety-sixth Street. The majority fall into the wide category of specialty shops, which means that they don't sell anything that you may particularly need, but do sell things that you didn't even know you wanted. For those looking to play a little mini golf, Buccaneer Golf is right on the border between the two towns.

THE BEACHES The beaches in both towns aren't that big, but they don't need to be, because the crowds rarely, if ever, reach the uncomfortable level. Prices for beach badges are very reasonable in both towns, $3 for the day, $7 for the week, and $13 for the season.

🍥 🍥 🍥

Two Towns That Wear Their History on Their Bathing Trunks

Ocean Grove

Ocean Grove is like no other Shore town in New Jersey, and for that matter, like no other place in the state. It is a living example of a Victorian planned community, with most of the buildings and structures dating back to the late 1800s. Originally called the Ocean Grove Camp Meeting Association, the town had a decidedly religious flavor; it was founded by a group of Methodists in 1869. Over the years, the religious flavor stayed intact, but in addition came tourists to check out the architecture and enjoy a peaceful respite in a quiet Shore town. The thriving Main Avenue shopping district has all types of stores and eateries.

The majority of visitors to Ocean Grove stay in one of the town's many bed-and-breakfasts. It's tough to find a summer rental here; many people are beginning to call Ocean Grove their year-round home.

Ocean Grove is not the best place to take the young-sters who might get a bit restless staring at even the eye-catching brightly colored and very decorative buildings and shopping in quaint stores all day, but the town is so charming that even the little ones might be able to take it for a day trip, which many families choose to do.

THINGS TO DO The shopping area abounds with stores that run the gamut from fancy to chintzy; it's a wonderful place to spend an afternoon. Of course, no visit to Ocean Grove is just about the shopping. The Great Auditorium is a must-see, and Tent City is an interesting little area to check out. There are over one hundred cloth tents huddled together with little cabins behind them. They are rented out each summer, but don't hold your breath if you want one; the waiting list is measured in decades. Ocean Grove also sponsors hundreds of events and concerts each summer, many of which are held in the Auditorium or nearby at the Boardwalk Pavilion. CALL 800-773-0097 OR GO TO WWW.OCEANGROVE.ORG FOR INFORMATION.

THE BEACH For a little romance, take a walk along the boardwalk in Ocean Grove. It's not a boardwalk with fun and games; it's just a boardwalk. But with the Atlantic crashing on one side and the charming town on the other, it's truly a beautiful setting. As for the beach itself, it's usually pleasantly uncrowded. The sand seems to be drifting

Ocean Grove Highlights

COLORFUL HOUSES

GREAT AUDITORIUM

TENT CITY

BOARDWALK PAVILION

out into the ocean, as in most northern Shore towns, but there's still plenty left to enjoy. The pricing is a little expensive: it's $5.50 for the day, $27.50 for the week, and $60 for the season.

Cape May

First things first, and I speak from experience here: Cape May is not for children, unless they're being punished. That said, allow me to say that Cape May is probably the single most charming place in all of New Jersey. The whole town is one giant Victorian-era romp, from the architecture to the trolley cars to the men walking around in stovepipe hats and such.

A lot of visitors to Cape May are seniors and couples getting away from it all for a weekend. You won't find many pizza shacks dotting the landscape, and you won't find much in the way of Camaros thumping down the road. You will find a plethora of fine dining, wonderful tours of the town, and a general feeling of relaxation pervading every step you take. For lodging, you would be remiss not to check in to one of the many bed-and-breakfasts in town.

A LITTLE HISTORY Cape May is generally considered to be one of the oldest (if not absolutely the oldest) seashore resorts in America; people have been coming to relax since the mid eighteenth century, which, obviously, predates America itself. Oh, the paradox. Such historical luminaries as presidents Lincoln and Grant vacationed here, and all was going along just fine until a fire in 1878 wiped out half the town. In a flurry of activity, the town was rebuilt within ten years, and the buildings you see today, those ubiquitous Victorian structures, were built during that time. Today, the town has National Historic Landmark status, which, if nothing else, means that there probably won't be too many Victorian McDonalds popping up. And, as an interesting aside, Cape May lies below the Mason-Dixon line, so a trip to Cape May means you're headed into southern country, albeit without crossing a state line.

The Chalfonte Hotel

THINGS TO DO Go sightseeing. Stop by the Mid-Atlantic Center for the Arts at 1048 Washington Street to pick up brochures and to sign up for guided tours. Many of the tours involve seeing the old estates, and some offer such extras as brunch and tea. There are also trolley tours, tours that take you out to sea, and tours that take you to the beach. After you tour yourself silly, you can do some shopping at the Washington Street Mall, an outside affair. The Washington Street area has served as Cape May's downtown for well over a century, and many of the touches from a bygone era remain, such as awnings that are hand cranked by the store owners to protect their merchandise from the sun.

THE BEACH The beaches at Cape May are slightly different from those along other parts of the Shore. For one thing, because of its geographical location (it's where the Atlantic Ocean and Delaware Bay converge), the sand can get awfully pebbly in spots. Other than that, the beaches are clean but on the smallish side. Perhaps the best beach in Cape May is Sunset Beach, located at the southern tip of our fine state. The beach itself is average—it's the amenities that make it a perfect place to spend an afternoon. Sunset Beach is aptly named for two reasons. First, it's located at the bottom of Sunset Boulevard. Second, for reasons only the sweet-natured folks at the Weather Channel can explain, you get to see the sun fall under the horizon at the end of the day in picture-perfect conditions. The horizon line is completely unobstructed, and apparently certain atmospheric conditions that are caused by sea breezes create a crystal-clear sky. While you're waiting for dusk, enjoy the bay beach, go hunting for Cape May diamonds, and do a little browsing at the shops right off the beach.

Don't miss the delightful experience of outdoor dining in Cape May.

🐚 🐚 🐚

Two Towns That Stay Up Late Enough for Last Call

Manasquan

Manasquan in the summer is Twenty-Something Central, much to the chagrin of year-round Manasquanians. In an attempt to slow the tide, many laws have been passed or are being proposed in an effort to inhibit the party-goers from turning the town into a regular Sodom and Gomorrah. Noise ordinances have been put in place, but the young and the restless still come to Manasquan for the sun, fun, and rum. There aren't all that many bars in town, but the lines outside O'Neill's at 390 East Main Street, the Osprey at Main Street and First Avenue, and Leggett's, a few paces past the Osprey, often wind around the block.

Lodging in Manasquan generally consists of house rentals. Group rentals are bread-and-butter for the realtors, and there's nothing quite like sharing a summer home with 247 of your closest friends, beer not included. Prices for these houses are surprisingly reasonable considering that there's rarely a vacancy.

THE BEACH The beach at Manasquan is frequented by mostly the young professional crowd, although there's a handful of families that remain unafraid of the youth. The southern end of the beach is considered to have some of the best surfing conditions in the whole state. Even if you don't surf, there's still plenty of Zen-style happiness to be experienced if by simply watching the surfers do their thing.

The pricing for the beach is as follows: $4 a day, $38 for the season for all except senior citizens, who can enjoy the pleasures of the beach at Manasquan for a mere $16.

Margate City

The city of Margate City, as it's officially known, is home to what may be the most interesting of all New Jersey's landmarks, Lucy the Elephant. Aside from Lucy, the town doesn't have a lot to offer the vacationer in terms of things to do, and that's just fine with the people who own summer homes there. On the beaches during the day and in the bars at night, it is a destination for the young and unattached, a great place to meet and greet members of the opposite sex, whoever the opposite for you may be. Although the town seems sedate, it sits in the shadow of Atlantic City and draws people from all surrounding towns in the evening.

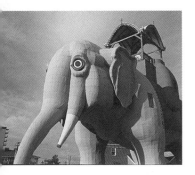

Lucy the Elephant looks better than ever.

THE BEACH The Washington Avenue beach in Margate is a great place to people-watch. If the urge does strike you, the prices for admission are $3.50 daily and $10 for the season.

Two Towns That Aren't Even Towns

Sandy Hook

Sandy Hook exists as a beach (albeit part of the federal Gateway National Recreation Area, which includes waterfront areas in New York and New Jersey), and a beach only. It is the quintessential day-tripper paradise. So of course the place gets packed to the gills every weekend as the northern folks hop on the Parkway, get off at Exit 117, go down Route 36, and set up shop for the day. You have to get there early, however. A certain number of cars are allowed access, and then that's it. So if you think you can roll out of bed at noon and expect to get in right after lunch, you'll be disappointed. If you enjoy late afternoon beach relaxation, however, by all means head over around four; the crowds thin out by then. In the beach season, the parking fee is $5 during the week and $10 on weekends.

The Sandy Hook beaches are your normal run-of-the-mill Jersey beaches, with Seagull's Nest a popular spot, if for nothing else than its concession stand. They are nice beaches, though; run-of-the-mill is pretty good in New Jersey. Also, they are extremely low-key in the way of dress, social stratification, how you look in a bathing suit, and so on. One spot stands out from the crowd—a stretch of sand known as Gunnison Beach, which is a clothing-optional enclave. It's generally considered bad form to remain in the cottons of summer once you're on this beach. For those of you who are inclined to let it all hang out in the ocean breeze, there's something you should know. The idea of a nude beach conjures up all sorts of bacchanalian pleasures, at least in my head, but the fact is that there aren't a lot of glamorous movie-star types skipping about. You're more likely to find people who remind you of your neighbors or your Uncle Harry and Aunt June spread out on a blanket.

A LITTLE HISTORY Sandy Hook is home to Fort Hancock, which during World Wars I and II was a strategically important stretch of beach. During World War II, it was assumed that if New York City were to be attacked, it would be through Sandy Hook, so bunkers and encampments and heavy artillery were scattered all about the

peninsula. After we won the war, the artillery was stored away wherever artillery is stored. Eventually, in 1975, the whole of Fort Hancock was turned over to the National Park Service, and we sun-worshippers gained full use of the Sandy Hook beaches. Today you can take a tour of Fort Hancock and see the buildings, all in various states of disrepair, as they stood in the not-so-distant past. The tour, unlike Gunnison Beach, is not clothing optional.

A nearby bluff more than 200 feet above the beach offers great views of Sandy Hook and New York City. The decommissioned lighthouse at Twin Lights Historic Site in Highlands, on the point of land between Sandy Hook Bay and the Navesink and Shrewsbury Rivers, dates to the mid-nineteenth century. It was the first lighthouse in the country to be powered by electricity and is now a museum of local maritime history.

Island Beach State Park

Island Beach State Park is one of the last undeveloped barrier beaches on the northern East Coast.

Island Beach State Park is the crown jewel of the Jersey Shore. Why? For starters, it's one of the last undeveloped barrier beaches on the northern East Coast. And that means no lights, no cameras, no action—just beach, dunes, marshes, and anything else that's been there since the dawn of humankind. Stretching out over 2,700 acres, the park is perfect for virtually any type of summer fun, from just plopping yourself down on the sand to scuba diving, picnicking, boating, birdwatching, hiking, and biking on the road that runs out to the end of Sandy Hook.

The park itself is divided into the northern and southern natural areas, with the recreational zone smack in the middle. The parking lot allows 1,850 cars, and closes when it hits that magic number, so do get there early. There is no shortage of nature trails to walk along, boats to rent, and fish to catch. Island Beach State Park is the perfect beach day trip.

~ ~ ~

*Twelve Towns and Beaches
That Don't Fit Any Category
But Are Too Much a Part of
Shore Lore to Leave Out*

Sea Bright

Sea Bright remains a popular spot for North Jerseyans to spend a day or a week. The town is small, with virtually all activity taking place along Ocean Avenue. Many of the beaches are private, which means that the beaches left for Joe Q. Public aren't exactly the cream of the crop. In fact, most of the beaches leave a little to be desired; they're small and cramped, which is not anybody's fault but nature's. There is a decent supply of restaurants to eat at and little shops to browse in. One of the main points of interest is the seawall, which keeps the town of Sea Bright from washing into the adjacent waters. If the Atlantic Ocean continues to rise, the wall will have to be built higher. And higher. And higher.

Long Branch

Since a fire destroyed Long Branch's pier in 1987, when the water slide, carnival games, and arcades went up in flames, there's been a slow regrowth for a town that was once—all before the 1920s—a summer hideaway for no fewer than seven presidents. The new Long Branch, the Long Branch that town planners hope one day to see, is anchored by the enormous Ocean Place Hilton Resort and Spa. The Spa offers pretty much anything you'd reasonably expect from a spa, including massages, mud baths, herbal body wraps, and Salt Glo Loofahs. Yes, that's right. Salt Glo Loofahs. The massages are certainly a highlight, and you get to change into a terry cloth robe and everything.

The beaches at Long Branch are not for the faint of heart.

The beaches at Long Branch are not for the faint of heart. As it has in many northern New Jersey Shore towns, the ocean has reclaimed copious amounts of sand from Long Branch's beach. The waves are made more for surfers than bathers, and that includes even the waves off the beach at Seven Presidents Oceanfront Park, which many consider to be one of the finest beaches in Monmouth County.

Deal

Deal is not a tourist town. Most of the beaches are dominated by seashore mansions, and people living in them don't take kindly to trespassers. And as far as things to do, well, your best bet may be bringing your own deck of cards. Deal has virtually zero tourist trade, and it doesn't need it, since it's New Jersey's wealthiest Shore town. Driving through, however, and looking at the mansions is fun—if you're a masochist who enjoys feeling deprived.

Asbury Park

Back in the 1920s, this town was bursting with civic pride. Wide, tree-lined streets. A marvelous boardwalk, complete with Convention Hall, which drew top performers from all over the world. It was a haven for middle-class families, a place where they could go and unwind for weeks at a time. A high time indeed. By the 1960s, however, things had changed. Other Shore towns were drawing on the tourist trade, years of neglect had started to wear through, and the downtown shopping district was being displaced by malls outside town.

Bruce Springsteen saved Asbury Park once. Will another celebrity come along and turn it around again?

Just when things were bottoming out, along came the Boss. Bruce Springsteen did for Asbury Park what the Beatles did for Liverpool, what Berry Gordy did for Detroit. He turned a depressed area into the center of the rock-and-roll universe. Convention Hall was hopping again. And of course there was the Stone Pony, the place where Bruce and company really put it on.

But like all things rock-and-roll, the impression lasted long after the scene ran its course. Asbury Park quickly fell back into the abyss. In the 1980s, there was a buzz that Asbury Park was on the verge of being turned into a giant theme park, with such backers as country superstars Johnny Cash and Willie Nelson and perhaps even the Jackson family ponying up the stones for the development. Obviously, it all fell flat.

Today, the beach area of Asbury Park resembles a ghost town. The Stone Pony, the last vestige of a time gone by, has closed its doors. All the old amusement areas have closed, and Convention Hall isn't convening anything.

All this bad news leads to a question. When will Asbury Park bounce back? Notice I'm not asking if. It's definitely a when proposition. After all, we're talking about beachfront property here. Some day somebody will take the time, effort, and risk involved to turn Asbury Park around. Any takers, Mr. Springsteen?

Avon-by-the-Sea

First, it's pronounced AH-von, as if your doctor were sticking a piece of wood down your throat, or maybe A-von, as in "can't." It is not AY-von, like the lipstick people. Now that that's been settled, Avon is a quiet community that apparently has no interest in attracting large numbers of people to its shores. It's a great place to spend a relaxing weekend away, though. The hotels and inns are small and comfy, and the beaches are sparkling, clean, and neat.

Sea Girt

Adjacent to Spring Lake, Sea Girt is that town's nontouristy cousin. It's virtually 100 percent residential, and the only reason to visit the town is if you know people who live there. The beaches are fine by any standard. One point of interest in town is a large white mansion, dubbed the Little White House, where past governors of New Jersey used to spend their summer vacations. It's not open to the public, so you'll have to admire it from the sidewalk.

Mantoloking

You think Bay Head is upper-crusty with little to do? Well then, you haven't visited Mantoloking. Huge homes dot the landscape, and if you don't own one of them, then there's precious little to do or see. The beaches are marvelous, but parking is difficult (in fact, there's virtually no place to park). All in all, a great town if you live there.

Seaside Park

Do not confuse Seaside Park with Seaside Heights. They are, despite the same first names, fourth cousins twice removed who haven't seen each other since Barry and Joan's wedding twelve years ago. Seaside Park is the perfect place to stay if you want the amenities of Seaside Heights without the noise. The chief difference in lodging is that beachfront motels face the ocean and an empty boardwalk in Seaside Park and not the crazy scene that is the boardwalk in Seaside Heights. Also, you're closer to Island Beach State Park, and that's a good thing anytime.

Barnegat Light

Located on the northern end of Long Beach Island, Barnegat Light is perhaps most famous for the lighthouse at the tip of the island. But there's more. For one thing, Barnegat Light boasts a proud fishing heritage, and it's interesting to head over to Viking Village on the bay side and watch the boats being loaded or unloaded for the day. Although it's becoming increasingly difficult to make a living from the sea, there are still people willing to try.

The town is a welcome respite from the hurly-burly that goes in the other towns on the island, and it tends to attract the same visitors year after year. There's plenty of food and drink to go around, and Rick's American Cafe is a popular destination. Play it again, indeed.

Barnegat Light shows its colors to tourists both on land and at sea.

Loveladies

Many towns stand out for their architecture, but Loveladies puts them all to shame. While many towns feature Victorian motifs, Loveladies could best be described as Beverly Hills chic. No two homes look alike. Jutting out at all angles, the homes in Loveladies, especially those on the beach, are marvels. And if you're lucky enough to own one or be vacationing in one, you won't be too disappointed to find out that there's not much to do within the town's borders. Ah, so what. You're in a cool house.

Ship Bottom

Ship Bottom is Long Beach Island's most traveled town, although by default. When you get off of the bridge leading to the island, you're right in the middle of Ship Bottom. Thanks to its easy access to the mainland, Ship Bottom has a decent-sized year-round community, which, also as a result, puts Ship Bottom in an interesting position. While it wants tourism dollars, it doesn't want them at the expense of its residents. So Ship Bottom has a little bit of every-thing—quiet areas, loud areas, restaurants, bars, hotels, homes, shopping. Not a bad place to visit, and you wouldn't mind living there. The town apparently got its name when, in the first half of the nineteenth century, a boat washed ashore, with, it seemed, no survivors. Then the people who came upon the ship heard a knocking from the ship's bot-tom, and out popped a lovely young woman.

Longport

Another ritzy town, this one is in the shadow of Atlantic City. Beautiful homes, great beaches, and quiet enjoyment are what residents and vacationers alike enjoy here. The architecture is a mix of the young and old, much like the population of the town itself. Even if you're not staying in Longport, it's worth a trip to the Longport Inn to sample the crab cakes.

CHAPTER II

BEYOND
THE BEACH

S itting on the beach day after day is enough
for some people. Others, like me, need
more variety to balance their days. Maybe it's
roller coasters that get your heart pumping,
or perhaps a day of fishing
is what you need. Whatever it is,
you're "Shore" to find it on
the Jersey coast.

Boardwalks and Other Beach Amusements

Going to the Shore doesn't have to mean going on a roller coaster every night, but let's face it. Boardwalks are fun.

BELMAR PLAYLAND, 1400 OCEAN AVENUE, BELMAR, 732-681-5115, also known as the Belmar Casino, calls itself a "family entertainment center," and it's open year-round.

There's a seemingly endless assortment of rides, games, food, and drink at the Seaside Heights Boardwalk.

With typical boardwalk fare like Skeeball and arcade games and the like, it certainly qualifies. There's a mini-golf course upstairs, and Lisa's Gourmet Ice Cream and Coffee is inside. There's also a "game" called Bessie, which to the untrained eye just looks like a regulation-sized cow, but is really a ticket-spewing monstrosity that you "milk" to get your hands on those tickets.

THE POINT PLEASANT BOARDWALK is full of good-time fun. It's dotted with the typical array of arcades and games of chance, and there's also an honest-to-goodness funhouse, complete with clowns and mirrors that make you look like a freak of nature. The standard rides are there—roller coasters and such—but not until you digest your food.

THE SEASIDE HEIGHTS BOARDWALK features a dizzying array of rides, games, food, and drink. It's impossible to take it all in at once.

THE FUNTOWN AMUSEMENT PIER (732-830-1591) and the CASINO PIER (732-793-6488) are where the rides are, and they have any flying metal contraption you could possibly think of. Roller coasters, merry-go-rounds, the Gravitron, everything. The Gravitron, for the uninitiated, is an enclosed, spinning space-saucer contraption that reaches speeds of something like 12,000 miles an hour and sticks you against the wall so that you can barely move a muscle.

LUCKY LEO'S ARCADE, 215 BOARDWALK (732-793-1323), is a haven for video games, Skeeball, and that machine that has all those quarters being pushed around by some unknown physical force, and the only way to get any tokens or tickets out of it is by explaining the theory of relativity to a blank-faced attendant, and all that will get you is a couple of sticks of incense. Lucky Leo's basically invented the boardwalk arcade; it's been in business nearly half a century. As the sign says, "We must be doing something right." Yes, Leo, you are.

WATER WORKS, AT SHERMAN AVENUE (732-793-6501), has giant slides and tubes where you reach speeds you didn't know were possible. Even if you're afraid to go shooting down a five-story slide, you'll still get a kick out of watching other people have the experience. Without fail, everyone who comes flying down the chutes ends up laughing and carrying on like an eight-year-old, whether they're eight or fifty-eight. People also spend some time at Water Works sitting around in beach chairs getting a righteous tan. A fun, fun way to spend an afternoon.

SAND TRAP MINIATURE GOLF COURSE, TWENTY-THIRD STREET AND LONG BEACH BOULEVARD, SHIP BOTTOM, 609-494-3185, is a mini-golf course that offers weekly tournaments.

SETTLER'S MILL ADVENTURE GOLF COURSE, 806 NORTH BAY AVENUE, BEACH HAVEN, 609-492-0869, is a mini-golf dream course, with waterfalls and bridges and genuinely difficult holes to navigate. And at each hole is a plaque detailing some history of Long Beach Island, so you can learn and have fun all at the same time.

FANTASY ISLAND, 320 WEST SEVENTH STREET, BEACH HAVEN, 609-492-4000. This is Beach Haven's answer to the boardwalk. The scene is reminiscent of the old-time town carnivals, with families and groups of teenagers mingling, eating cotton candy, going on the Tilt-a-Whirl, trying to win a stuffed *South Park* charac-ter. Fantasy Island has a roller coaster and a water park, and shows for children, too. This is what sum-mer is all about.

PLAYLAND'S CASTAWAY COVE, BOARDWALK AT 10TH STREET, OCEAN CITY, 609-399-4751, creates the classic Shore setting: basically, a bunch of kids pestering their parents to give them money so they can play games and go on rides and get cotton candy in their hair. In other words, summer. Playland's Castaway Cove features the Python, Ocean City's only loop-the-loop roller coaster.

PARK PLACE, 5000 PARK BOULEVARD, WILDWOOD, 609-522-3300, bills itself as a family entertainment center, and it is just that, offering two "adventure" mini-golf

You won't need your golfing gear to enjoy the Shore's miniature-golf delights.

courses, batting cages, an arcade, pizza, ice cream, and a brand-new roller rink. Park Place stands out from the crowd by being away from the crowds. It's not located on the boardwalk, so you don't have to fight through throngs of people to play Pac-Man.

MOREY'S PIER AND THEME PARKS, WILDWOOD, 609-522-3900, stand out among the best amusement parks at the Shore. The three parks combined boast seven world-class roller coasters (including the world-famous Great White), two water parks, four go-cart tracks, a phalanx of games, and more rides than any other park in the world. Each of the three piers has its own personality. The pier at Twenty-fifth Street is the most action-packed, the Schellenger is more family-oriented, and the Spencer pier, with the new Doo Wopper roller coaster, has a 1950s feel. There is really no experience quite like walking the Wildwood boards on any evening in the summer.

There is really nothing like riding, walking, and crossing the Wildwood Boardwalk in summer.

DINOSAUR BEACH ADVENTURE THEME PARK, POPLAR AVENUE AND BOARDWALK, WILDWOOD, 609-523-1440, WWW.DINOSAURBEACH.COM. This is what you'll find there: lots of rides, lots of games, lots of fossils. We're not talking about some plastic fossil-like stuff here. We're talking gen-u-ine fossils. One interactive attraction at Dinosaur Beach is known as the Fossil Dig, where you actually go searching for the aforementioned fossils. Sponsored by the Academy of Natural Sciences, it brings a little post-Jurassic fun to the Shore. Not so incidentally, some of the newer rides are bone-tingling, such as the Crazy Mouse, a wild roller coaster in which the car you sit in spins around while it runs roughshod over the tracks. Another quaint little joy ride is the Rocket, which shoots you up eighteen stories by going from zero to sixty miles per hour in two seconds and then drops you back down in free fall, creating a sense of weightlessness. And probably nauseousness.

Gone Fishin'

Fishing is available all over the place for the able and not-so-able angler in us all. Whether you decide to fish from a jetty, right off the beach, or up the road, the opportunity exists to catch any fish you feel like catching. Probably the best bet is to hop aboard one of the many boats that take out to sea for a day of angling. Here's a sampler.

BELMAR MARINA, ROUTE 35, BELMAR, 732-681-2266, is known clunkily as the "Home of New Jersey's Largest Charter Fishing Fleet," or, for those who need an acronym, HNJLCFF. As you might expect, it's a boat haven. It overlooks the Shark River and is filled to the gills with fishing and party boats that run 365 days a year, 366 in leap years. Call for boat schedules and other pertinent information.

DAUNTLESS, BROADWAY BASIN, 47 BROADWAY, POINT PLEASANT BEACH, 732-892-4298, makes two trips daily. The 7:30 AM departure is mostly for sea bass, porgies, and flounder; it returns at 3 PM. The night trip, which runs from 7:30 PM to 12:30 AM, is mostly for Jersey blues in season, but an occasional tuna may nibble your line.

Fishing is available up and down the Shore for the angler in us all.

NORMA-K FLEET, KEN'S LANDING, POINT PLEASANT BEACH, 732-899-8868, features three big boats measuring 95, 75, and 70 feet respectively. They're not only for people who fish, mind you, but for everyone, with fireworks cruises debarking every Wednesday and Thursday at 8 PM and regularly scheduled romantic moonlight sails.

SEA GYPSY, BEACH HAVEN YACHT CLUB, ENGLESIDE AVENUE AND THE BAY, BEACH HAVEN, 609-492-2843/2896. Captain Ed Lemke will takes you out for a half or full day of fishing for blues and tuna.

MISS BARNEGAT LIGHT, EIGHTEENTH STREET AND BAYVIEW AVENUE, BARNEGAT LIGHT, 800-325-SEAS, is for the serious bluefish fan. The blue may be the fiercest fight, pound for pound, in the Atlantic. If you don't feel like fishing, check out the upper deck, where, it's slyly noted, "bathing suits are welcome."

ROYAL FLUSH, 6100 PARK BOULEVARD, WILDWOOD CREST, 609-522-1395, has three trips daily, so you don't have to get up at the crack of dawn to enjoy some time on the high seas. The Monday and Friday afternoon trips are "Ladies' Days," with women paying half fare.

FISHING ADVENTURER II, WILDWOOD MARINA FISHING CENTER, 609-729-7777, bills itself as Wildwood's family-fun boat. It offers two trips during the day and an eight-hour evening bluefishing cruise.

ρ ρ ρ

Won't You Let Me Take You on a Sea Cruise?

If fishing isn't for you, here are some cruises that may be.

If you don't want to catch fish, what about a sea cruise?

RIVER BELLE SAILS FROM THE BROADWAY BASIN, 47 BROADWAY, POINT PLEASANT, 732-528-6620. It offers lunch, brunch, and dinner cruises, pizza and fireworks cruises, and special cruises on holidays. The New Orleans–style boat travels on the calm waters of the Manasquan River, Point Pleasant Canal, and Barnegat Bay. There's usually a deejay on board, so feel free to come with me, to the sea, the sea of love. The *River Belle* sails from mid-April through New Year's Eve; call for official times and dates.

BLACK WHALE III SHIPS OUT OF MORRISON'S MARINA, BEACH HAVEN, 609-492-0333. It offers a variety of cruises. You can take the inland route, which will take you through Little Egg Harbor Bay and right to the Trump Marina Casino, if gambling is your thing. You'll get cocktails and live entertainment on that trip. In the evenings, there's a bay sightseeing cruise, and on this trip the children on board are given a chance to steer the hundred-foot behemoth of a boat.

WILD GOOSE IS BASED AT THE SUNSPLASH MARINA, 228 BAY AVENUE, OCEAN CITY, 609-398-7075. There are four trips daily, and they're meant to be educational as well as fun, with lectures to enlighten you about what you're seeing. The various trips will take you out to the bay, the ocean, or both.

For a whale (or dolphin) of a time, hop aboard the **BIG BLUE CRUISER—WHALE WATCHER,** 4500 PARK BOULEVARD, WILDWOOD, 800-246-9425, 609-522-2919. There are three daily cruises: 10:30 AM for dolphins, 2 PM for whales and dolphins, and a 7 PM sunset cruise (which is a wonderful way to end the day). Seeing a humpback whale jumping out of the water or a bottlenose dolphin zipping along is truly a special experience. While there are no guarantees, the captain claims a 75 percent spotting rate on the trips. There is a naturalist on board to answer any questions you may have about the marine and other wildlife you'll encounter on your cruise.

CAPE MAY WHALE WATCHER, MISS CHRIS MARINA, THIRD STREET AND WILSON DRIVE, CAPE MAY, 800-786-5445, bills itself as "New Jersey's largest and fastest." It offers several whale watches: the highlight of the operation would have to be the dinner cruise and dolphin watch. Call by 4 PM, give your dinner order, show up at the marina before the boat sets sail at 6:30 PM, and off to the waters you go. They guarantee that you'll spot dolphins.

"Aye aye, Captain," you'll feel like saying when you board the **YANKEE SCHOONER,** OCEAN HIGHWAY DOCK BETWEEN WILDWOOD AND CAPE MAY, 609-884-1919. A big ol' sailboat that looks as if it was plucked right out of some Errol Flynn flick, the Yankee Schooner has daily cruises, including an afternoon "Sunlovers' Delight" and a sunset cruise. Call for reservations. Something smaller: For a peaceful ride through Cape May's back bay salt marshes, stop off at **MISS CHRIS MARINA,** CAPE MAY, 609-884-3351, and they'll set you up with what you need, namely a kayak.

Whoop-Whoop-Whoa-Zow-Eeeeee-Yikes

Just because you're on vacation doesn't mean your heart can't pump like Secretariat. Check out these thrill-a-minute rides.

SHARK RIVER WATER SPORTS, 618 FIFTH AVENUE AT MAIN STREET, BELMAR, 732-681-3383, is the place to go for Jet Ski and kayak rentals. It's the only place in town that gets you in the ocean, as opposed to the bay. You'll find one-, two-, and three-person Jet Skis and one- and two-person kayaks.

ISLAND SURF AND SAIL, 3304 LONG BEACH BOULEVARD, SHIP BOTTOM, 609-494-5553, is another place for buying or renting kayaks and windsurfing material. It offers lessons as well.

For ninety minutes of exhilaration, check out the **SILVER BULLET,** WILDWOOD MARINA, 609-522-6060. It's the world's largest speedboat, measuring seventy feet from stem to stern, and it shoots you out into the water at speeds approaching breakneck. From there, it's time for a little whale and dolphin watching, and then a zoom back to Shore. Wear clothes that you won't mind sitting in wet. Better still, wear a bathing suit, because the sea spray will get you. Call for reservations.

What do you get when you cross a parachute, a motorboat, and a healthy dose of fearlessness? You get parasailing, one of the most exhilarating experiences you can have five hundred feet in the air. **PARASAIL, INC.,** WITH LOCATIONS AT TWO MILE LANDING, OCEAN DRIVE, WILDWOOD, 609-522-1869; EIGHTY-EIGHTH STREET AND THE BAY, SEA ISLE CITY, 609-263-5555; AND THIRD STREET AND THE BAY, OCEAN CITY, 609-399-3559, will take you high above the seashore for a view and a feeling you just can't get anywhere else.

Tame and Dry

After the bouncing cages on the Ferris wheel and the salt spray of a the sightseeing boats, you may be in the mood for some on-the-ground dry-land activity. Think bike ride, whether you bring your own bicycles from home or rent them at any one of numerous places up and down the coast.

Aside from the occasional sand dune and sea wall, the Jersey Shore is flat (although you may be surprised at the extent to which head winds and crosswinds can make even a flat oceanfront ride feel like a climb). Even with breezes, the Shore offers terrific riding for the whole family. In the off season, boardwalks make great bike paths; of course, they're popular with bikers in the summer, too, but there's a lot of foot and pedal traffic. The same could be said of any of the temptingly flat roads and streets along the Shore. Long Beach Island is a great place to go for a long, flat, and scenic bike ride, from Old Barney to the architectural delights of Loveladies and the relatively unheralded Victoriana of Beach Haven, but it's a lot more relaxing to do that ride in September than on a busy beach day in July. Here are just a few other especially appealing routes.

SANDY HOOK Even in summer, you can ride a bike into Gateway National Recreation Area without paying a fee (the fee is for motor vehicle parking). The problem is, in summer there is a lot of car traffic, and bicycling may not be as pleasant as it is in early fall–or any other time of year. You can pick your route and riding distance within the park, and stop at such attractions as the Spermaceti Visitor Center and the buildings at Fort Hancock.

ISLAND BEACH STATE PARK The eight-mile road through the park is scenic, with constant views of unspoiled barrier beach.

OCEAN CITY BOARDWALK From tricycles to training wheels to tandems, this is another of those places where people love to ride.

> Sun on the sand, wind whistling over your bike helmet, a level path, and tangy salt air. That's bike riding at the Shore.

Mom! I'm Bored!!!
I Said I'm Bored!!!

The sweet sounds of children fill the air...or, the unrelenting imperatives of children fill the air. Either way, children are filling the air, and they need things to do. They can attempt to build sand castles for only so long. Here are some fun things to do with the kids, and you might have fun yourself.

Jenkinson's Aquarium boasts touch tanks, sharks, seals, penguins—and a great candy shop just next door.

Our old friends, the Jenkinsons, invite you to check out the aquarium that bears their name. **JENKINSON'S AQUARIUM,** PARKWAY AND OCEAN AVENUE, POINT PLEASANT BEACH, 732-899-1212, is the place to be to check out all things aquatic. There are touch tanks, sharks, seals, penguins—and you're allowed to feed the animals, so to speak, at certain times throughout the day. Have you ever fed an alligator? Here's your big chance. For $6.50 for adults and $4.00 for kids, who could pass up the opportunity to meet Seaquin the seal eye-to-eye? Situated indoors on the boardwalk, the Aquarium is a great respite from the hot sun.

At **JENKINSON'S BEACH,** every summer Monday at 7 PM brings the kiddie beach show, featuring (and changing by the week) everything from magic to pony rides. And every Tuesday is the kiddie concerts on the beach. These and other child-oriented activities are held right on the beach.

JUST BEAD IT, with three locations on Long Beach Island, all on the Boulevard: 1616 IN SURF CITY, 609-494-8177; 2707 IN SHIP BOTTOM, 609-494-6020; AND 203 IN BEACH HAVEN, 609-492-BEAD, is an ideal spot for the little-girl set. Pick your string, pick your beads, and start making necklaces and the like. You can string them together there or take home a bunch to do at the kitchen table.

BAYVIEW PARK, SIXTY-NINTH STREET, BEACH HAVEN, is a bayside beach for preschoolers. The swimming area is fenced in, and there's also a playground with a seesaw and jungle gym.

THE BEACH AT BAYVIEW AVENUE AND TWENTY-FIFTH STREET, BARNEGAT LIGHT, is another place for small children to swim in the peaceful waters of the bay. The swimming area is fenced in, and the play area features a six-car wooden train for the engineer in us all. The train makes only one stop, unfortunately, and it did that many years ago.

AREA 54, ON THE PROMENADE BETWEEN SEVENTH AND EIGHTH STREETS, OCEAN CITY, 609-399-TAGI, sounds like something out of *The X-Files,* and it kinda-sorta is. Featuring laser tag and virtual reality, it's open all day and well into the night for family fun, if you consider shooting a laser gun at your mother to be family fun.

OCEAN CITY AQUARIUM, 1119 ASBURY AVENUE, OCEAN CITY, 609-398-2255, is famous for its sharks, too many to count. There's also a touch pool where you can get your hands wet petting the marine life, and you can even touch a real live shark (completely safe, they say). As a precaution, count your fingers before you stick your hand in, and then count them again after. You can't be too careful.

MARKET DAYS, DOWNTOWN OCEAN CITY, EVERY THURSDAY, 10 AM–1 PM. Why it's called that, I don't know. What it is, however, is a collection of face-painters, a balloon artist, jugglers, and musicians who descend on the 600 to 1000 blocks of Ocean City each week. A great way to start a day, and the price is right: free.

Ocean City's Market Days feature face-painters, balloon artists, and more.

Shore History 101

You didn't think the Shore was just about sand and surf, fun and games, did you? There's a rich history behind (and along) the dunes, and stopping off at some of the following places can give you a taste of yesteryear.

BARNEGAT LIGHTHOUSE STATE PARK, BARNEGAT LIGHT, 609-494-2016. A trip to Long Beach Island is not complete without a stop at Old Barney the Friendly Lighthouse, located at the northern end of the island. Getting to the top of Old Barney means climbing 217 steps. (If you suffer from vertigo or recently had arthroscopic surgery on your knees, it might be best to sit this one out.) But the views of the water and Island Beach State Park are tremendous, and the whole scene surrounding the lighthouse is different from virtually any other along the Shore.

The park also has picnic tables, a thousand-foot walkway for fishing (not to mention sitting and walking), a great spot for bird-watching (especially in the fall and winter), and a fraction-of-a-mile nature trail through the remnants of one of the last maritime forests in New Jersey. The beach is sparkling white sand, but no swimming is allowed in the park.

The Ocean City Historical Museum has a large collection of antique toys.

THE LONG BEACH ISLAND HISTORICAL ASSOCIATION, ENGLESIDE AND BEACH AVENUES, BEACH HAVEN, 609-492-0700, has a museum filled with artifacts from days gone by. It also offers walking tours and a Monday night lecture series featuring such topics as "Gunning Clubs and Yacht Clubs on LBI."

THE OCEAN CITY HISTORICAL MUSEUM, IN THE COMMUNITY CENTER, 1735 SIMPSON AVENUE, OCEAN CITY, 609-399-1801, features displays such as the Victorian Rooms, decorated as they were a century ago. It also has a large collection of toys, fashions, and pictures.

LUCY THE ELEPHANT, 9200 ATLANTIC AVENUE, MARGATE CITY, 609-823-6519. Lucy sits majestically overlooking the beach. Certainly one of New Jersey's, if not the world's, curiosities, Lucy stands 65 feet high and was built in 1881 by a developer hoping to attract potential homeowners to the Shore. Since then, Lucy has served as a summer residence, a tavern, and a landmark. Today, you can head in through one of her hind legs and investigate her for yourself.

THE ATLANTIC CITY HISTORICAL MUSEUM,

BOARDWALK AT NEW JERSEY AVENUE, ATLANTIC CITY, 609-347-5837, offers up a history of the "queen of American resorts." With the help of pictures and artifacts dating back to the mid-1800s, you'll be able to trace the trajectory of Atlantic City's rise, fall, and resurrection. Once inside, you'll quickly recognize that few other cities have gone through as many changes in a single century as Atlantic City has.

HEREFORD INLET LIGHTHOUSE, FIRST AND CEN-

TRAL AVENUES, NORTH WILDWOOD, 609-522-4520, is on the National Registry of Historic Places, as well it should be. Dating back to the mid-nineteenth century, the lighthouse has withstood winds, rains, and the displacement of light-keepers, not to mention virtually complete disrepair. But today, the lighthouse is back in action, and plans to turn part of it into a nautical museum are continuing. Throughout the summer, the lighthouse sponsors craft shows and boasts beautiful gardens. If you're getting married, the lighthouse grounds are available for your ceremony, either on the grounds or in the gazebo.

THE EMLEN PHYSICK ESTATE, 1048 WASHINGTON

STREET, CAPE MAY, 609-884-5404, is one of the great Victorian showplaces of the region. It doubles as the home for the Mid-Atlantic Center for the Arts, which rescued it it from disrepair. It houses the personal belongings of a family that once lived there; you can visit the luxurious "upstairs" world of the family and the "downstairs" world of the servants. There are living-history tours throughout the summer; call for details.

The Emlen Physick Estate is one of the great Victorian showcases of the region.

THE CAPE MAY LIGHTHOUSE, LIGHTHOUSE

AVENUE, CAPE MAY POINT, 609-884-5404, was also rescued by and is now operated by the Mid-Atlantic Center for the Arts. It was built in 1859, the third lighthouse to occupy the point. After you climb the 199 steps to the top, you'll be greeted by actors portraying Harry and Belle Palmer, the last keepers of the light. There are historical exhibits about Cape May on the stair landings as well as at the top, so you won't be bored if you stop to rest in the midst of your climb.

It's Time for Some Culture

Don't you want to enrich your soul and your senses? Here are some opportunities to encounter culture at the Shore without experiencing culture shock.

5

Music, Art, and More

CONCERTS AT THE GREAT AUDITORIUM IN OCEAN GROVE

MORE CONCERTS AT THE BOARDWALK PAVILION, ALSO IN OCEAN GROVE

CLASSES AT THE LONG BEACH ISLAND FOUNDATION FOR THE ARTS AND SCIENCES

SURFLIGHT THEATRE

OCEAN CITY POPS

Attempting to list all the cultural events in Ocean Grove would be like attempting to list all the noncultural events in Seaside Heights–there's more than anyone could possibly catalog. Many of the events take place in OCEAN GROVE'S GREAT AUDITORIUM, a 6,500-seat, mostly wooden structure that in its century-plus history has seen some of the most important religious, political, and entertainment figures of the times speak or perform there. The list includes Helen Keller, Paul Robeson, Bob Hope, the Reverend Billy Graham, Andrew Carnegie, and seven presidents, including New Jersey's almost-own Woodrow Wilson; and the hills (dunes, maybe?) came alive when Maria Von Trapp traipsed through.

But the past is past, and as Ocean Grove moves into the twenty-first century, the culture just keeps on a-comin'. Besides the Great Auditorium, the BOARD-WALK PAVILION is the other place to catch the best of what Ocean Grove has to offer. Last summer's list included concerts by Neil Sedaka, the Glenn Miller Orchestra, and the Dukes of Dixieland. You could also have participated in a checkers tourney or enjoyed a spot of tea at the annual Teddy Bear Tea in the Garden.

THE LONG BEACH ISLAND FOUNDATION OF THE ARTS AND SCIENCES, 120 LONG BEACH BOULEVARD, LOVELADIES, 609-494-1241, offers classes all summer long on subjects such as "sculptural basketry," where you'll start with an "interesting piece of driftwood" and end up with a "one-of-a-kind basket." The classes really do run the gamut, from drawing and painting to "fabulous fish printing." If you haven't printed a fabulous fish, well, you're missing quite a scene.

THE SURFLIGHT THEATRE, ENGLESIDE AND BEACH AVENUES, BEACH HAVEN, 609-492-9477, has been hosting shows for close to half a century. It's first-rate stuff at the Surflight, with productions put on by New York actors who, once they get their roles, make LBI their home for the summer. As an added treat, you can usually find the same actors hanging around outside during the day, practicing their lines.

The season runs from March until December, and the Surflight presents about fifteen shows a year.

For close to three-quarters of a century the **OCEAN CITY POPS** have brought symphonic treats to the Music Pier at the Boardwalk. Concerts range from big brass bands to the best of Broadway to a night at the opera. Without a doubt, they provide the finest in musical entertainment down the Jersey Shore. CALL 609-398-9585 OR CHECK OUT WWW.OCEANCITYPOPS.ORG FOR INFORMATION ABOUT THE SUMMER CONCERT SERIES.

THE GREAT AMERICAN TROLLEY COMPANY, WILDWOOD, 609-884-7400, doesn't have San Francisco's legendary hills, but it's fun to ride anyway. The Wildwood Island route is active year-round; in summer the trolleys also go to the Cape May bus station and to Cold Spring.

HISTORIC COLD SPRING VILLAGE, 720 ROUTE 9, CAPE MAY, 609-898-2300. Cold Spring Village shows you Cape May as it was in the nineteenth century, and offers some good shopping, too. From there, you can hop aboard the Cape May Seashore Lines Passenger Trains for a stop at the Cape May County Park and Zoo. That's only one tour; there are many others. Call for descriptions, schedules, and prices.

Natural Wonders

The Shore was full of life even before there were people around to make history and music and artifacts. After all, we're not the only ones who like the beach. The Shore abounds with wildlife, and here are three great places to appreciate it.

The stated goal of the **MARINE MAMMAL STRAND-ING CENTER,** BRIGANTINE BOULEVARD, BRIGANTINE, 609-266-0538, is the rescue and rehabilitation of stranded or stressed marine mammals and sea turtles. Since 1978, when the center opened, it has rescued more than 1,500 whales, dolphins, seals, and sea turtles. Think of it as *E.R.* for marine life, only without the romantic complications. The Center has rescued everything from a five-pound Kemps Ridley sea turtle to a twenty-five-ton whale. While size is not an issue when responding to calls, it does become one if the mammal must be brought back to the Center for rehab. Mostly, it's seals and dolphins that are taken back to the Center, where they are cared for until they are ready to be released back into the wild. In 1978, the year the Center first started, it responded to nineteen calls. In 1993, with nets and boats and other hazards for mammals becoming increasingly prevalent, there were 123 strandings.

If you go to the Center, you'll receive a free tour and lecture that runs approximately half an hour. The facility is tiny and easily missed. It's located about a hundred yards before the Lighthouse Circle on Brigantine Boulevard. Call for information and to report sightings of stranded marine mammals. THE CENTER ALSO HAS A GREAT WEB SITE AT WWW.MMSC.ORG.

THE WETLANDS INSTITUTE, 1075 STONE HARBOR BOULEVARD, STONE HARBOR, 609-368-1211, is a testament to the growing concern for wetlands preservation. There is plenty to learn about here, with exhibits, laboratories, and natural habitats providing hands-on learning opportunities. The Institute exists, as its mission statement says, to "promote appreciation and understanding of the vital role wetlands and coastal ecosystems play in the survival of life on this planet." It truly is a beautiful place as well, with six thousand acres stretched across the coastal wetlands. While you're there, you can check out the panoramic view from the observation tower or take a hike along the Salt Marsh Trail.

The knobbed whelk is New Jersey's very own state seashell.

THE NATURE CENTER OF CAPE MAY, 643 WASHINGTON STREET, CAPE MAY, 609-884-9590, is an environmental education facility for the whole family. Situated in Cape May Harbor, it not only provides access to the beach and marshes but also offers workshops, walking tours, and exhibits such as the Tidal Marsh Tour. And be sure to bring binoculars for bird-watching.

Nine Types of Seashells You Might Find at the Shore

You don't need a nature center to appreciate nature. All you have to do is walk along the beach. There are more than seventy-five varieties of shells that you might be able to track down on a Garden State beach, but the nine listed at the right are the most common. (Incidentally, though it's not on this list of shells you're likely to find, New Jersey has its very own state shell: the knobbed whelk–basically, a large snail shell.) The best times to go seashelling are at low tide and after summer storms, which works out well, since those are also great times for a general-purpose walk along the beach.

🐚 🐚 🐚

Shop 'Til You Drop, Then Crawl

What would a vacation be without some shopping? The Shore is packed with every type of shop, with surf shops and gift/handicraft/everything-you-want-but-don't-need shops dominating the landscape. Some of the best of them are listed here; so are some shops that are a little bit off the beaten path.

THE RUBBER STAMP ACT, 1005-1/2 MAIN STREET, BELMAR, 732-681-7441, sells more than five thousand different rubber stamps, from Happy Birthday images right up to, and including, Miss Piggy. The stamps generally sell for five to eight dollars, and you can also have rubber stamps custom made if you ever get the urge to emblazon your family crest on your stationery.

NOSTALGIC NONSENSE, 903 MAIN STREET, BELMAR, 732-681-8810, is a little slice of Greenwich Village in Belmar. It sells both new and used "retro" clothes and virtually everything else that, for better or worse, has that groovy 1970s look attached to it, such as a John Travolta picture-postcard book. Welcome back, welcome back, welcome back.

FLY AWAY KITES, 1108 MAIN STREET, BELMAR, 800-29-KITES, bills itself as the largest store devoted to kites on the East Coast. If it has to do with kites, this place has it covered,

9

Shells at the Shore

ATLANTIC JACK-KNIFE CLAM

ATLANTIC OYSTER DRILL

ATLANTIC SURF CLAM

BLUE MUSSEL

CHANNELED WHELK

COQUINA

EASTERN OYSTER

NORTHERN MOON SNAIL

AND, OF COURSE, THE NORTHERN QUAHOG (YOUR BASIC CLAM)

right down to kite clothing. The shop also offers a free kite clinic on the beach for those of us whose kites have fallen ill. Or maybe they teach you how to keep those darned things in the air.

If you have spent at least one waking moment on this earth, you have probably been inundated with all things Disney—theme parks, television shows, movies, and who knows what else. You also have probably stepped inside a Disney store in your favorite mall. Well, for a more peaceful Disney shopping experience, allow me to direct you to **MICKEYLAND,** 56 MAIN AVENUE, OCEAN GROVE, 732-988-5495. It sells the typical array of Disney-themed stuff, such as toys, figurines, greeting cards, games, whatever your little Mickey heart desires. IT ALSO OFFERS MAIL ORDER, AND YOU CAN E-MAIL THE STORE AT ITS WONDERFUL ADDRESS: GOOFY4ALL@AOL.COM.

THE TIME MACHINE, 516 ARNOLD AVENUE, POINT PLEASANT BEACH, 732-295-9695, is, as they say, pure nostalgia. Or, as they also say, a "pop culture extravaganza." I feel confident that they have everything that you could possibly want. Note that I didn't say "need," but "want." For starters, there are tons of records dating back to the 1950s. Need Shaun Cassidy's latest 8-track? Probably there. Need a *TV Guide* from 1963 to complete your collection? No prob. A Betamax machine? Coming right up. Atari 64 cartridges? Mm-hmm. It's a pop culture bonanza. And when you discover how much those little *Star Wars* figures you used to buy at Toys 'R' Us cost now, and then realize that the shiny black Darth Vader storage case propped up next to them is worth more empty than what you paid for the whole collection back in the 1980s, you will decide never to throw anything away again. Ever. It will change your life.

THE POINT PLEASANT ANTIQUE EMPORIUM, BAY AND TRENTON AVENUES, POINT PLEASANT BEACH, 800-322-8002, features more than a hundred antique dealers ensconced under one roof. It's for buyers and for sellers, and it offers all types of antiquey stuff, from lamps to clocks to furniture to your Aunt Betty's fine china. The building that houses the emporium looks spacious and elegant when you walk up to it, and the interior lives up to that promise.

THE JOLLY TAR, 56 BRIDGE AVENUE, BAY HEAD, 732-892-0223, is everything a Shore town store should be. What will you find there? Lamps with bases made of seashells, watercolor paintings of seascapes, and, most impressively, a collection of original photographs dating back to the 1880s of Bay Head and surrounding beach towns. The Jolly Tar also offers, in no particular order, china, stuffed animals, mailboxes, and a wedding service that does it all, from invitations to receptions.

MRS. DUFF'S GIFT SHOPPE, 614 LONG BEACH BOULEVARD, SURF CITY, 609-361-8400, nets you all the Shore knickknacks you can shake a stick at, including candles, snow globes, welcome signs, and everything else Shore-related.

KATHIE'S SURF CITY SMOKE SHOP, 1715 LONG BEACH BOULEVARD, SURF CITY, 609-361-1403, Surf City is a one-stop cigar lovers' paradise, with every type of cigar imaginable.

THE SEA LIFE GALLERY, 1715 LONG BEACH BOULE-VARD, SURF CITY, 609-361-8400; ALSO 2900 DUNE DRIVE, AVALON, 609-368-7300. This is an art gallery that just might eat up all your vacation money. The gallery has some truly breathtaking examples of artistry. For instance, out front sits (swims?) a $32,000 bronze dolphin. Inside are more bronzed marine life figures, as well as original paintings and prints. The highlight for me personally is the no-maintenance fish tank—complete with fish that require, as advertised, no maintenance. Of course, the fish aren't real, but hey, you can't have everything.

THE KITE STORE, 313 LONG BEACH BOULEVARD, SURF CITY, 609-361-0014, WWW.THEKITESTORE.COM, is a, well, kite store, selling kites for beginners and up. You can also purchase windsocks and flags here to decorate your home.

RON JONS SURF SHOP, 201 NINTH STREET, SHIP BOTTOM, 609-494-8844, is the place to go for all summer clotheshorsing. This store has it all, so mentioning all the shirts, shorts, bathing suits, surfwear, and so on would just be repetitive and boring. So no mention will be made of the hats, surfboards, suntan oils, or cool necklaces either.

Beach Buys

KITES

BOOKS

HAWAIIAN SHIRTS

LEATHER

CHRISTMAS
ORNAMENTS

MORE BOOKS

SNOW GLOBES

A BRONZE
DOLPHIN

THE BOOKSTORE, 7901 LONG BEACH BOULEVARD, BEACH HAVEN, 609-494-1224, is, as its name suggests, a bookstore. Now virtually every beach town has its own bookseller, and Borders and Barnes and Noble dot the New Jersey landscape like orange highway barrels, so why mention yet another little bookseller? Well, it's the prices. This is a used-book store, and every paperback is $1.25. In the mood for romance? Those panting Harlequin novels can be had for $1.49–for six of them.

OOH-LA-LA, 13211 LONG BEACH BOULEVARD, BEACH HAVEN, 609-492-5252, WWW.OOHLALACRAFTS.COM, is chock-full of 100 percent handcrafted goods, from clocks to menorahs to chopsticks, metals, ceramics, textiles–you name it. More than three hundred different artists are featured at any given time.

SCHOONER'S WHARF, 325 NINTH STREET, BEACH HAVEN, 609-492-4400, is like a little mall, with beachy stores dominating the landscape. Two stores stand out: the Toy Safari (you figure it out) and Surburbia, which, despite its name, is not a one-stop shop for vinyl siding and lawn jockeys but a hip, hip joint for the skateboarder in us all. Imported CDs, posters, clothes, and the like are what this place is all about.

> At the Bookstore in Beach Haven you'll find an abundance of paperbacks for perfect beach reading at bargain prices.

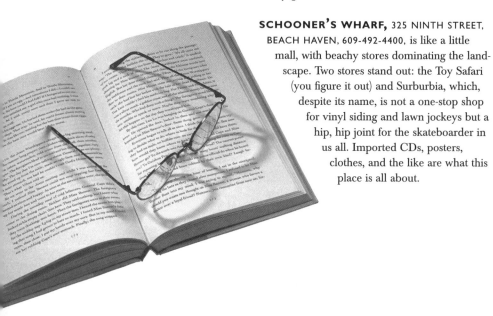

RIC'S ALOHA CLASSICS, 213 BAY AVENUE, BEACH HAVEN, 609-492-8896, is a classic surf shop. When I say "classic," I mean it's not some chain touting the latest styles, but an honest-to-goodness hardcore surf shop. For example, the Hawaiian shirts are made in Hawaii. They also have a ton of old surfing magazines and videos, surfboards, Kona coffee, those wood sculptures known as Java Men, and numerous surfing-related CDs. The Endless Summer begins here.

THE MOD HATTER, 8071 BAY AVENUE, BEACH HAVEN, 609-492-0999, sells hats—derbies, king's crowns, baseball caps, Indiana Jones–style hats, Sherlock Holmes–style hats, Dr. Seuss *Cat in the Hat* hats, hats for style, hats for substance, hats to keep you dry, hats to keep you cool. They're the Mod Hatter. They sell hats.

THE CUSTOM LEATHER SHOP, 601 NINTH STREET, OCEAN CITY, 609-814-1002, is a place to let your inner cowboy ride. Featuring boots, jackets, belts, wallets, and just about anything else that can be made of leather. It's not a classic Shore stop, but "Yee-Haw!!" anyway.

Ho-ho-ho, Merry...August? At **CHRISTMAS ISLAND,** 400 MADISON AVENUE, CAPE MAY, 609-884-4343, you can pick up all your Christmas needs any time between June and December. Holiday soap? They've got it. Festive ribbon? Yes. "But do they have sand-dollar ornaments?" I can hear you asking. The answer to that is a sincere "You betcha."

CHAPTER III

EAT, DRINK, AND BE MERRY

What do you really remember about a vacation? You'd like to think it's the great weather, or the day you learned to dive without splashing, or the afternoon your third-grader won a sand-castle-building contest. And all those things might well be part of the picture in your mind, but you'll almost certainly remember the food, too. It may very well be a boardwalk stroll, custard cone in hand, or a dinner overlooking a Cape May sunset, that comes most vividly to mind in a dull moment of a gray November day.

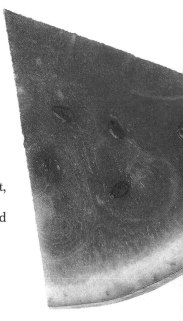

Start the Day Right: Best Breakfasts

It's been said by many nutritionists, health care professionals, and mothers, and I don't dispute it, "Breakfast is the most important meal of the day." After a night of restful sleep, your body is just begging for some protein and carbohydrates to get the motor running. Of course, some people can get by on their nicotine, caffeine, and sugar fix, but we're not one of them. We're strong, we're healthy, and we're probably not eating lunch until 2 PM. With all this in mind, find the closest place on this list, pick up the morning paper, take a walk, and enjoy one of the best breakfasts at the Jersey Shore.

WALLY MITCHELL'S, 712 LONG BEACH BOULEVARD, SURF CITY, 609-494-1667, is perennially a winner of some random Best Breakfast award or another, and it's a popular morning spot. The Eggs Benny, as you might expect from the cute nickname, consists of poached eggs on a toasted English muffin with ham and hollandaise sauce—how can you go wrong? Keep in mind, though, that you can leave your American Express card at home, and all other credit cards for that matter. Cash only.

At the Bagel Bank, you an make a mouthwatering withdrawal every day.

BAGELS AND BEYOND, 1616 LONG BEACH BOULE-VARD, SURF CITY, 609-494-4848, has won Ocean County's Best-Bagels Election a number of times (who votes for these things, I don't know, but that's what the sign out front says). It helps, of course, that the bagels are big and doughy, just the way they should be.

CAPTAIN JOHN'S MR. BREAKFAST, NINETEENTH STREET, SURF CITY, 609-494-0924, is a favorite among locals, as you can tell by the general seaworthiness of the clientele. Basic fare, quick service.

THE CHICKEN AND THE EGG, 207 NORTH BAY AVENUE, BEACH HAVEN, 609-492-FOWL, does not claim to know which did indeed come first. You can try to figure it out yourself with the signature dish, the Chicken or the Eggwich, which is breast of chicken, egg, and cheese on the ever-present Kaiser roll. The breakfast menu boasts

eleven different omelettes and all other types of breakfasty
stuff, such as waffles and pancakes. In addition to the popular breakfasts, the Chicken and the Egg has a lunch and
dinner menu, although the huge lines of hungry customers-
to-be usually form between 9 and 10 AM.

THE BAGEL BANK, 3301 BAY AVENUE, OCEAN CITY,
609-398-7728, features eighteen different types of cream
cheeses to spread on your bagel. My personal fave is the
Veggie Garlic. Open from 6 AM, the Bank prides itself on
baking bagels (and croissants, muffins, brownies...) fresh each
day. In addition to the breakfast menu, the place also serves
up some tasty sandwiches and salads.

MALLON'S, with three locations in Ocean City, one in
Sea Isle City, and one in Avalon, is quickly becoming a
Jersey Shore tradition. Open only since 1988, Mallon's has
created quite a stir with its homemade sticky buns. It's not
unusual to see lines trailing out the front door of its shops as
people wait, salivating over what's to come. The Mallon's at
1340 BAY AVENUE, OCEAN CITY (609-399-5531) is open
from Easter to Christmas; the rest operate only in summer.

**BRIAN'S WAFFLE HOUSE AND FAMILY RESTAU-
RANT,** 2408 DUNE ROAD, AVALON, 609-967-3058, is the
place to see and be seen in the morning hours. Featuring
the All-Star Breakfast Special–a glass of orange juice; two
eggs anyway you like 'em; three pancakes; your choice of
cholesterol in bacon, ham, or sausage; coffee or tea–all for
a flat fee of six dollars. Brian's slogan, "Where mornings
begin," sounds like a commercial for freeze-dried coffee,
but, in this case, it rings true.

THE RUSTY RUDDER, IN THE BEACH TERRACE
MOTOR INN, OAK AND ATLANTIC AVENUES, WILDWOOD,
609-522-3085, offers what may be the biggest breakfast buffet in all the world. Hyperbole aside, it has more than seventy items to choose from, and that doesn't include the
Top o' the Morning Bloody Mary. There's also a dinner
buffet, with "over 85 feet of food."

THE MAD BATTER, 19 JACKSON STREET, CAPE MAY,
609-884-4619, is the best place for pancakes on the Jersey
Shore. The only way to describe good pancakes is "fluffy,"
and that really doesn't tell you too much. So all I can say
is that if you're in Cape May, the Mad Batter is the place
for breakfast. Period.

**Whether your
breakfast choice
consists of
bacon
and eggs,
pancakes and
syrup, or even
brownies, you
won't go hungry
in the morning
at the Shore.**

Seafood, and Only Seafood

The Shore offers up some great seafood, and are there choices! Whether you enjoy an ultracasual atmosphere or can't eat seafood unless accompanied by a jacket and tie, the Shore has a restaurant that fits the bill (and one whose bill will fit your budget).

ZELBE'S, 506 MAIN AVENUE, BELMAR, 732-681-7887, offers seafood shack–type food quickly and deliciously. The utilitarian spirit is alive and well, signaled by a sign that proclaims, "Not fancy, great food, large portions, low prices." Yes, yes, yes, and yes.

THE YELLOW FIN, TWENTY-FOURTH STREET AND LONG BEACH BOULEVARD, SURF CITY, 609-494-7001, is a newer dining establishment that puts a new twist on the traditional seafood menu, featuring daily specials and delectables from its very own pastry chef. The prices are reasonable, and the decor is yellow (!) and bright.

BEACH HAVEN FISHERY, TWENTY-SECOND STREET AND LONG BEACH BOULEVARD, BEACH HAVEN, 609-492-4388, is, for my money, the best seafood that LBI has to offer. The place isn't fancy, and the food comes in a Styrofoam box, but it's perfect. The Beach Haven Fishery's mission is to ensure the quality of the fish, making sure it's fresh, making sure that it's prepared perfectly. They have it all, but the stated dish du jour is always John's Blushing Shrimp, which is large shrimp sautéed in fresh tomatoes, herbs, and garlic, and then crusted with bread crumbs and Parmesan cheese. Too fancy? Then grab the best crab-cake sandwich on the island.

The M&M Steam Bar promises, "If it swims, we've got it."

M&M STEAM BAR, DELAWARE AND THE BOULEVARD, BEACH HAVEN, 609-492-9106, is an open-air fish market/eatery where the emphasis is on food, not decor. The seafood, however, is delicious, and the wry humor is delectable. Their motto: "If it swims we've got it, if it smells, we've had it too long." All summer long, you'll see people sitting outside the block-long eatery, enjoying everything from steamed Dungeness crabs to Maine mussels.

SEAFOOD GARDEN, 8611 LONG BEACH BOULEVARD, BEACH HAVEN, 609-492-8340. The food's the thing here. A sample dish: Grannie's Key West Shrimp Royal, with plump Gulf shrimp topped with butter, Parmesan cheese, lime juice, garlic, and toasted crumbs, all in a dish of tri-colored pasta. Go ahead. I dare you to stay away.

HARVEY CEDARS SHELLFISH COMPANY, EIGH-TEENTH STREET AND LONG BEACH BOULEVARD, HARVEY CEDARS, 609-494-0088, is a classy, laid-back, wooden-table joint. The portions are barely finishable, the waitstaff is knowledgeable, and the food is just great. Forget for a moment that you're not supposed to eat fried foods, and wallow in the combination platter, a nongreasy, lightly fried feast of sea scallops, deviled crab cake, flounder, and butterflied jumbo shrimp.

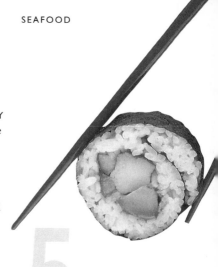

THE BOATHOUSE RESTAURANT, RIO GRANDE AVENUE, WILDWOOD, 609-729-5301, sits right over the water, and the great food is just part of the whole deal here. You can sit in the dining room or on the open-air deck to enjoy a fine dinner, or, if you're feeling more casu-al, grab a seat on the Dockside Crab Deck for lunch or a light dinner. Enjoy a drink, watch the sun set, relax.

BOOKERS NEW ENGLAND SEAFOOD HOUSE, NINTH STREET AND WESLEY AVENUE, OCEAN CITY, 609-399-4672. This family-owned and -operated establishment specializes in, yes, seafood. Be careful not to load up too heavily on the free salad and appetizer bar before you enjoy the main course.

THE LOBSTER HOUSE, ON, IN, OVER, AND AROUND FISHERMAN'S WHARF, CAPE MAY, 609-884-8296, is special for many reasons, not the least because it's one of a handful of restaurants on the East Coast that operates its own fishing fleet. Needless to say, you don't have to worry about the freshness of the food you'll be eating, whether you sit down in dining room, take a load off at the raw bar, grab a quick bite in the cocktail lounge, or purchase a lobster feast to go. The lobster will be one of the best you ever had.

FIVE GREAT SUSHI RESTAURANTS What does sushi have to do with the Shore? Not much. Except that sushi is seafood, and seafood comes from the ocean. See my logic? Granted, not everybody enjoys this delicacy, but for those who do, the list at the right tells you where to go. The food at all five places is delicious, but sushi tastes begin and end with your personal taste buds, so check these restaurants out and enjoy.

5
Top-Notch Sushi

ENGLESIDE SUSHI BAR
ENGLESIDE INN
30 ENGLESIDE AVENUE
BEACH HAVEN
609-492-5116

UMI
701 BLACK HORSE PIKE
PLEASANTVILLE
609-407-2121

HARUMI'S ICHIBAN
944 BOARDWALK
OCEAN CITY
609-399-4244

TOKYO PALACE
135 LONGPORT-
SOMERS POINT BOULEVARD
SOMERS POINT
609-927-8650

KUISHIMBO
330 NINETY-SIXTH STREET
STONE HARBOR
609-967-7007

Ice Cream

It doesn't matter whether you're with your kids, your grandparents, or your significant other. It doesn't matter if you're big or small, short or tall. All that matters is that everybody likes ice cream, and what better place to enjoy all its milky goodness than at the Shore?

BEACH PLUM HOMEMADE ICE CREAM, 420 MAIN STREET, BRADLEY BEACH, 732-776-9122, serves up thirty-six different flavors in an old-style setting, with the roof creating a huge awning over picnic tables.

DORCAS RESTAURANT AND SODA FOUNTAIN, 58 BRIDGE AVENUE, BAY HEAD, 732-899-9365, is in a building that dates back to 1880. The food is generally of the burger variety—it's the ice cream you want to stick around for. You have to pass through a screen door to enter, and the "Soda Fountain" part of the name is not just for show. One ice cream highlight is the Black Cow, which is two scoops of vanilla plopped into a root beer. And to enjoy it while sitting on a white swivel stool is sublime.

THE SUNDAE TIMES sits majestically at 17 ATLANTIC AVENUE, SPRING LAKE, 732-974-1236. Built of brick with monstrous columns, it looks like a miniature White House. The sundaes are all named for newspapers, such as the *New York Times,* the *Star-Ledger, USA Today,* and so on. The Kelly-green-and-white decor is very ice creamy, and there are forty-one flavors of that milk and cream delight, along with four flavors of yogurt, three sherbets, and two ices.

RALPH'S ITALIAN ICES, 600 GRAND CENTRAL AVENUE, LAVALLETTE, 732-854-0800, also serves up some great ice cream, despite not telling you that in its name. Thirty flavors, milkshakes, and the like. Look for the dancing lemon in a top hat and bow tie.

SHOW PLACE ICE CREAM, 204 CENTRE STREET (AT BEACH AVENUE), BEACH HAVEN, 609-492-0018, is across from the Surflight Theatre, and it's probably the only ice cream place in the galaxy that has sittings. If you walk by it at night, it looks like a Russian bread line. The attraction? Well, the ice cream is good, but the play's the thing. A singing waitstaff, little skits, and audience participation (whether you like or not) are what make a visit to the Show Place a must-do event. If it's raining during the day there are three matinee shows. La-la-la.

SWEET NOTE ICE CREAM SHOP, SCHOONER'S WHARF, OFF NORTH BAY AVENUE AND TENTH STREET, BEACH HAVEN, 609-492-6827, specializes in ice cream and Belgian waffles. Another favorite is the Caramel Cashew Turtle, which, I'm told by those who love it, is not actually a turtle. The Sweet Note is a small place, but perfect for that cone-to-go.

CAFE VACIO, 1511 LONG BEACH BOULEVARD, BEACH HAVEN, 609-492-7702, is a great coffee-and-cake place. The interior is inviting (best described as modern-homey), and, best of all, Wednesday night is S'mores Night–you get your graham crackers, marshmallows, and chocolate served to you on a platter, complete with the fire in the middle and skewers to roast with. If the urge to break out into "Hello Mudda, Hello Fadda," seizes you, it's understandable

Ice cream, yogurt, sherbet, and ices— not to mention the extras. Who needs food?

THE HOBBY HORSE ICE CREAM PARLOR AND CAFE, EIGHTH AVENUE AND OCEAN DRIVE, OCEAN CITY, 609-399-1214, has forty-two flavors of ice cream and frozen yogurt; it also has cookies, pies, coffee, espresso, cappuccino, and those delicious chocolate-dipped strawberries and bananas. Feeling frisky? Order Marc's Mega Sundae, which will deluge you with five scoops of ice cream, three toppings, whipped cream, and, yes, a cherry on top.

JAKE'S ITALIAN WATER ICE, 1213 ASBURY AVENUE, OCEAN CITY, 609-814-0900, is a one-stop shop for water ices, gelati, soft custards, sundaes, shakes, and virtually any other cool summer treat.

TORY'S, 3308 ASBURY AVENUE, OCEAN CITY, 609-391-7933, is a throwback ice-cream shop. You walk in and an aura of old-time fun surrounds you. It claims to have ice cream, food, and fun, and it's accurate on all three counts.

DUFFER'S, 5200 PACIFIC AVENUE, WILDWOOD, 609-729-1817, serves up forty flavors of homemade ice cream and mixes up the finest milkshake this side of paradise.

Pizza

It might be lunch, it might be dinner, it might be a snack.
It might even be breakfast. It's pizza, and it can be found
everywhere on the Jersey Shore. Luckily for us pizza
lovers, pizza is a relatively healthy treat. You get your
grains, your dairy, and your veggies—it's almost a square
meal by itself. Of course, you can destroy the healthy
aspects of it by wolfing down a whole pie of the sausage-
pepperoni-ham double-cheese combo variety, but let's all
show some restraint here and eat like humans.

MIKE'S PIZZA, SEVENTEENTH AND OCEAN AVENUE,
BELMAR, offers the best slice in town. It's on your way
from the beach, so you won't need to call ahead. The
best part?The cheese stays with the dough. No mozzarella running down your wetsuit at Mike's. The sauce is
zesty, and the picnic benches out front offer the finest
in people-watching.

JOEY TOMATOES PIZZA, AT JENKINSON'S BOARD-
WALK, POINT PLEASANT BEACH, is another fine beach-
snack pizza establishment, with all types of pizza, including, yes, a tomato pie.

FAMOUS LOU MICHAELS RESTAURANT, 2901
LONG BEACH BOULEVARD, SURF CITY, 609-494-8900,
features delectable thin-crust terra-cotta pizza and offers
up pasta and ice cream as well as the pizza with a
"Brooklyn attitude"—brothers Lou and Michael's words,
not mine.

PANZONE'S PIZZA, BETWEEN ELEVENTH AND
TWELFTH STREETS, BEACH HAVEN, 609-492-5103; TWEN-
TY-SECOND STREET, SURF CITY, 609-494-1114, is perhaps
the most well-liked pizza joint on all of Long Beach
Island. It's won best-pizza awards all over the state,
from the local island newspapers right on up to the big
daddy of restaurant ratings, yes, *New Jersey Monthly*
magazine. The big draw, in my opinion, is the crust. It
tastes as if it's been lightly fried; of course, it hasn't
been, but the taste is très magnifique.

VIC'S, 60 MAIN STREET, BRADLEY BEACH, 732-774-8225,
has been serving up fine food for over fifty years. In fact,
on my visit there, I spoke with an old-timer who claimed
to have walked from Ocean Grove regularly in his youth
just to get Vic's pizza. The pizza is much like Bradley

Beach itself—nothing fancy, but darn good. Be fore-
warned, however: You can't just get a slice. The best
they'll do for you is a mini-pizza. As an added bonus,
there's a fine selection of beer and wine to chase down
your pepperoni.

MARUCA'S TOMATO PIES, 1927 BOARDWALK, SEA-
SIDE PARK, 732-793-0707, has been serving up the slices for
something like half a century. You owe it to yourself to
sample a slice.

MR. D'S PIZZA, STEAKS & SUBS, 4711 NEW JERSEY
AVENUE, WILDWOOD, 609-522-2026, has the best pizza in
all the Wildwoods. If you don't agree, your taste buds are
obviously malfunctioning.

UP AND DOWN THE BOARDWALK IN OCEAN CITY you
will find the famous **MACK AND MANCO'S PIZZA**
purveyors. The white pie is what everybody talks about,
but all the pizza is top-notch.

Lunch

The coffee and bagel you inhaled for breakfast can take
you only so far. It's lunchtime now, and those hunger
pains are stitching up your sides. Leave the umbrella in
the sand, grab your wallet, and go find something to hold
you until dinner.

MAX'S HOT DOGS, 25 MATILDA TERRACE (AT OCEAN
AVENUE), LONG BRANCH, 732-571-6797. A visit to Long
Branch without a stop at Max's is tantamount to high trea-
son. We're talking hot dogs whose size can make you
blush. We're talking beer on tap. We're talking history. The
place, in one form or another, has been around since 1928.
Although hot dogs are the bread-and-butter here, there are
also all kinds of burgers, chicken, and the like to
choose from. But those hot dogs! Nothing like
them. Don't forget to check out the Wall
of Fame, which is a veritable who's
who of entertainers, from
Springsteen to Sinatra to
Norman Fell, aka "Mr. Roper"
(you know, the landlord from

**And of course
there are
always
hot dogs.**

Three's Company). Hundreds of autographed eight-by-tens make for an interesting sidelight.

THE RASPBERRY CAFE, 60 MAIN AVENUE, OCEAN GROVE, 732-988-0833, serves up fresh salads and sandwiches with a a California bent. We're talking broccoli pitas and avocado sandwiches here, folks. There are some less healthy meals offered, such as a traditional B.L.T., but overall this is a place for the health-conscious. The Raspberry Cafe also serve up juices, coffees, and the ubiquitous smoothies, my favorite being the Blue Gardenia, a mix of orange juice, blueberries, and bananas.

Or you might be in the mood for conch fritters with lime aioli.

THE MIDWAY STEAK HOUSE, WEBSTER AVENUE AND BOARDWALK, SEASIDE HEIGHTS, 732-830-2666, signals the relative midpoint of the Seaside Heights boardwalk. It may also signal to your stomach that it's time for a sausage-and-pepper sandwich although your brain is saying no in no uncertain terms. Well, forget the brain here, folks. It's a good sandwich. You just ate a sausage-and-pepper sandwich? Well, tomorrow you can come back here and have a cheese steak.

SAW MILL RESTAURANT AND TAVERN, 1807 BOARDWALK, SEASIDE PARK, 732-793-1990, is near the Funtown Pier. It's another Seaside landmark. You can get a hamburger, cheese, and pork roll concoction, aka the Lumberjack, for four bucks. Cold beer on tap, too.

FOODIES CATERING, 8010 LONG BEACH BOULE-VARD, HARVEY CEDARS, 609-494-4214), offers virtually everything in the way of delicious food. And every single item is homemade, right there on the premises. If you're throwing a beach bash for a hundred of your closest friends, you'll find that picking the food off the massive seven-page, single-spaced menu might just be the single most difficult endeavor you'll undertake. (Can't decide between jumbo lump mini–crab cakes with cognac dill sauce or Key West conch fritters with lime aioli? Those are just the first two things mentioned on the menu.) If your party is going to be smaller, say, for just yourself, you might want to pick up a Foodies Beach Box, with two mini-sandwiches, cookies, and fresh fruit. There may be no better food stop on the planet.

SUBS & SUCH SANDWICH SHOPPE, THIRTEENTH STREET, BEACH HAVEN, 609-492-7114, offers up some of the biggest and tastiest subs this side of the Hudson (or the

Delaware, depending upon which city shapes your expectations). Consistently voted the island's best by residents and vacationers, Subs & Such is the place for a late-afternoon lunch.

THE WHISTLE STOP, SIXTH AND BAY AVENUES, BEACH HAVEN, 609-492-1580, has a menu that's as large as an elephant with an overactive pituitary gland. From burgers to hoagies to ice cream, the Whistle Stop is the place to go for a quick bite when you don't know exactly what you want.

THE WHITE HOUSE, 2301 ARCTIC AVENUE, ATLANTIC CITY, 609-345-1564, is the place to get a sub sandwich in Atlantic City. The White House bakes its own bread daily, and the sandwiches are thick enough to cause your jaws to lock in submarine ecstasy.

The White House bakes its bread daily, and that's just the beginning.

🌀 🌀 🌀

Stuff You Know You Shouldn't Eat, But You Can't Help Yourself

Indulge yourself. You can go back to melba toast and cottage cheese after your vacation.

CHIPPY'S FRESH FRENCH FRIES, 411 BOARD-WALK, POINT PLEASANT BEACH, 732-295-9617, serves up heaping portions of that newfangled creation made by putting sliced potatoes into canola oil and frying them to succulent perfection. For $5.49, a large batch of Chippy's finest will stave off your hunger for hours.

STUTZ CANDIES, 1419 LONG BEACH BOULEVARD, SHIP BOTTOM, 609-494-5303. This shop is a dentist's nightmare (or dream, depending on the ethics of your particular D.D.S.). Specialties include chocolate mint bark and almond butter crunch.

COUNTRY KETTLE FUDGE, NINTH STREET AND BAY AVENUE, BEACH HAVEN, 609-492-2800, AND TWENTIETH STREET AND THE BOULEVARD, SURF CITY, 609-494-2822. These shops offer fine hand-whipped fudge. If you walk into one of them and take a whiff, I'll bet you'll walk out with a bag of fudge under your arm. The places radiate fudgy goodness.

JOHNSON'S POPCORN, 1360 BOARDWALK, OCEAN CITY, 609-398-5404 (and additional seasonal locations on the Boardwalk), has been the popcorn emporium of the Shore since 1940. The caramel popcorn, of course, is the house specialty, and no self-respecting popcorn fancier could live without one of Johnson's T-shirts.

RAUHAUSER'S OWN MAKE CANDIES, 721 ASBURY AVENUE, OCEAN CITY, 609-399-1465, is yet another in the Shore's long, legendary line of sweetshops. Most of the sweet yummies here are homemade, including those colorful little gumdrop-like candies in the shape of bears. For more adult tastes, Rauhauser's also makes fudge.

SHRIVER'S SALT WATER TAFFY AND FUDGE, NINTH STREET AND THE BOARDWALK, OCEAN CITY, 609-399-0100), is the only place in town that makes saltwater taffy, and it's been doing that for a long time. Shriver's recently celebrated its hundredth anniversary. Stop in and pick some up, or perhaps enjoy some fat-free fudge.

STEEL'S FUDGE, 1000 BOARDWALK, OCEAN CITY, 609-398-2383; 2719 BOARDWALK, ATLANTIC CITY (609-345-4051). Steel's has been in the fudge business since women wore full-length dresses on the beach. Eat fudge.

If you love popcorn, prove it with a Johnson's Popcorn T-shirt.

HANKINS' CANDIES, 3012 PACIFIC AVENUE IN WILDWOOD, 609-522-8438, gives you an offer you can't refuse: Buy one pound of fudge, get a second pound free. Dentist bills not included.

STEAK KING & PIZZA, 25TH STREET AND THE BOARDWALK, WILDWOOD, 609-729-1637, is open until the wee hours and, get this, offers free delivery. A late night BLT? No problem. With a menu that has every type of food you shouldn't be eating, the Steak King will probably reign over Wildwood for years to come. With a $4.95 spaghetti-and-meatballs special, who's going to challenge the King?

FRALINGER'S ORIGINAL SALT WATER TAFFY, with locations in Atlantic City, Ocean City, and Cape May, has been in business since 1885. All the taffy is made at the company's factory in Atlantic City.

HOT FRESH

JAMES' ORIGINAL SALT WATER TAFFY STORES,
with multiple locations, including Wildwood, Stone
Harbor, and three locations on the Boardwalk in Atlantic
City, is another traditional source of saltwater taffy. Save
the pink ones for me.

🌀 🌀 🌀

Dinner for Two (or Four, or Six, or Eight, or Everyone You Appreciate)

Can't decide between seafood and hamburgers? Not in the
mood to make a thousand choices? The following restaurants offer a little bit of everything.

MOONSTRUCK, 57 MAIN AVENUE, OCEAN GROVE, 732-
988-0123, is an Italian grill right in the middle of town.
Chances are you'll hear some Dean Martin while you're
enjoying your antipasto. And you will enjoy the antipasto—it's a colorful display of fresh mozzarella, red and
green veggies, and a bonus dab of pesto. The rest of the
menu is equally appealing.

THE DRAUGHTING TABLE, 416 MAIN STREET,
BRADLEY BEACH, 732-774-1044, can best be described as
a moderately upscale bar and grill. The menu offers traditional American fare, from sandwiches to such specialties as the Cajun Seafood Stew. The beer selection is
huge, and, perhaps most important, every Saturday night
brings the stylings of the Waterfront Duo singing top
motown, doo-wop, and R&B standards from yesteryear.
A little Smokey Robinson with your smoked turkey?

CHEF ED'S, 400 OCEAN AVENUE, BELMAR, 732-280-
0444, offers eclectic selections from land and sea in a very
casual atmosphere. You can sit inside or out, with a view
of the ocean right across the street.

OLD MILL INN, OLD MILL ROAD, SPRING LAKE, 732-
449-1800, is where you'd go for a fancy dinner out with the
family. Dine inside or out, with a lakeside view, in this former
gristmill. There's live music every night, and sometimes you
can dance, too (call for an entertainment schedule).

THE BAYOU CAFE, 209 FIRST AVENUE, MANASQUAN, 732-223-6678, brings the flavor of New Orleans to Manasquan. It's a brightly lit restaurant; all types of beads and other paraphernalia decorate the place.

O'NEILL'S BAR, GRILL, AND GUEST HOUSE, 390 EAST MAIN STREET, MANASQUAN, 732-528-5666. This is probably the best place on the Shore for a young, hip, child-less couple to spend a weekend. The sprawling guest house has more than fifty air-conditioned rooms, with no televisions. Once you manage to get past that hurdle, the place is as charming as a prince. The restaurant arm of the operation features numerous chef's specialties and seafood, as well as a Sunday brunch. The bar area fills up on the weekends, so except for going to the beach during the day, leaving the guest house is really not necessary.

THE CRAB'S CLAW, 601 GRAND CENTRAL AVENUE, LAVALLETTE, 732-793-4447, offers up some fine dining and drinking at reasonable prices. Shirts and shoes, regrettably, are required.

THE TERRACE TAVERN, 3201 LONG BEACH BOULE-VARD, BEACH HAVEN, 609-492-9751, is the type of place that can dress its waitstaff and bartenders in Hawaiian shirts and get away with it. The unstated theme is distinctly Jimmy Buffett, and any parrothead would feel right at home here. The bar is lively, the jukebox is rockin', and the food, from sandwiches to weekly seafood specials, is great. And yes, they do offer a "cheeseburger in paradise," known as the Paradise Burger. See you in Margaritaville.

TONY'S BALTIMORE GRILLE, 2800 ATLANTIC AVENUE, ATLANTIC CITY, 609-345-5766, serves up delicious Italian fare at ridiculously low prices. It's the type of place where you'd sit with your back to the wall while your moll impishly smokes her cigarettes, if that's the kind of guy you are.

THE SINDIA RESTAURANT, 801 PLYMOUTH PLACE, OCEAN CITY, 609-399-1997. Named after the nineteenth-century ship that sank off the Ocean City coast, Sindia serves some of the most sumptuous food at the Shore. The menu changes daily, and although the specialty is seafood, Sindia offers meats and pastas as well.

THE CAPTAIN'S TABLE, HOLLYWOOD AVENUE ON
THE BEACH, WILDWOOD CREST, 609-522-2939. There's a
soft spot in my heart for the Captain's Table. When I was
but a mere lad, my family often took a week's vacation in
Wildwood, and we went to the Captain's Table often. This
a family restaurant par excellence. "The only thing we
overlook is the ocean," they say, and they're right. The
food is good, the prices reasonable, and it's a haven for
harried parents. With a tableside magic show with dinner
on selected nights, and what the restaurant calls the
ASAP Survival Kit (kids get their food within ten
minutes), this oceanside dining establishment can't
be beat.

KOKOMO'S, 480 WEST RIO GRANDE AVENUE,
WILDWOOD, 609-523-1800, offers up great pasta,
steaks, and seafood in a tropical atmosphere. The big
draw, however, is its microbrewery, the only one in
Wildwood. You can see the large vats that hold the hops
and yeast and assorted other beer-making ingredients, then
see the bartender pour you a large glass of the freshest beer
imaginable.

RUSSO'S, 4415 PARK BOULEVARD, WILDWOOD, 609-522-
7038, is what an Italian restaurant should be. Family-owned
and -operated since 1922, Russo's strives to be sure that
Mama's recipes are being followed to the last pinch of
oregano. The menu features Italian basics such as veal
parmigiana and sausage scallopine. Russo's is a must stop
for fans of good Italian food–in other words, everybody.

410 BANK STREET, 410 BANK STREET, CAPE MAY, 609-
884-2127, is considered one of the finest dining establishments
in the state. The food is a mixture of French, New Orleans, and
Caribbean cuisines, and reservations are most certainly recom-
mended. Mesquite grilled lobster tail, anybody?

VAN SCOY'S BISTRO, CARPENTER SQUARE MALL,
CAPE MAY, 609-898-9898. For those of you whose middle
name is "I like eclectic food," Van Scoy's is the place to go.
Some featured menu items include prime rib Bangkok,
crab-stuffed mushrooms, and, of course, marinated tofu.

Bars and Clubs and Drinking and Dancing

BAR ANTICIPATION, 703 SIXTEENTH AVENUE, SOUTH BELMAR, 732-681-7422, or, as it's better known to its denizens, Bar A. It draws a mixed bag–from the preppy, hair-parted-to-the-side types of guys to those who tend to remove their shirts while dancing. With live bands and dee-jays mixing it up, dancing is always an option, but certainly not required in order to have a good time. There are tons of bars, and the "backyard" area looks as if it came directly from *Beach Blanket Bingo*. There's a beach volleyball setup, sand all over place, and Bar A even has beach chairs.

JASON'S JAZZ AND BLUES, 1604 MAIN STREET, BEL-MAR, 732-681-1416, is, much as its name suggests, a hep-cat jazz-and-blues establishment. In order to keep the riffraff to a minimum, a sign out front tells you that after 8 PM, collared shirts are required. Muddy Waters might not approve, but such is life.

D'JAI'S OCEANVIEW BAR AND CAFE, 1803 OCEAN DRIVE, BELMAR, 732-681-5055, is first and fore-most a place to get down and boogie. We're talking dancing, here, and with reggae, funk, and retro nights, it's not too difficult to get out there and shake your mon-eymaker. On weekends and most weeknights the place is packed to the gills.

THE OSPREY HOTEL, 201 FIRST AVENUE, IN MAN-ASQUAN, 732-528-1800, is known more for the bar than for the hotel. It grabs the young and unattached for nights of drinking and debauchery, dancing and singing to a deejay during the week and live music on weekends.

MARTELL'S SEA BREEZE, 308-310 BOARDWALK, POINT PLEASANT BEACH, 732-892-0131. This restaurant and its Tiki Bar bring the South Pacific to the North Atlantic. Martell's features live bands and partying both inside and out. Part of the outside deck is located right out over the ocean, where I'm sure many a summer romance has bloomed.

CLUB XS, 406 BOULEVARD, SEASIDE HEIGHTS, 732-830-3036, is a dance club where the young congregate on any given night. Tight-fitting clothes are the only thing to wear. Like, totally.

EJ'S, BOARDWALK AT SHERIDAN AVENUE, SEASIDE HEIGHTS, 732-793-4622, opens its doors at ten in the morning and doesn't close until two the next morning. A long day of drinking indeed. At night, it's a fun place, with jukebox music and pool tables. During the day, it's a fun place, with jukebox music and pool tables. Hey—it's a fun place.

YAKETY YAK CAFE, 408 BOULEVARD, SEASIDE HEIGHTS, 732-830-1999, specializes in 1950s-era dance music. Slick back your hair, guys. Break out the bobby socks and poodle skirts, ladies.

THE HUDSON HOUSE BAR, 19 EAST THIRTEENTH STREET, BEACH HAVEN, 609-492-9616, has a pool table, dartboard, jukebox, and the obvious: beer, wine, liquor. Check your pretensions at the door and kick back. It's a good old-fashioned honky-tonk, and I mean that in the best way possible.

Think martinis, not beer, at the Merion Inn's bar.

THE SEA SHELL MOTEL AND CLUB, 10 SOUTH ATLANTIC AVENUE, BEACH HAVEN, 609-492-4611, boasts one of the finest Happy Hours on the whole Shore. The back deck of this motel-based bar packs them in like sardines in a tin, and the parade of beautiful people is nonstop. Once Happy Hour ends, the place is empty. But then, at nightfall, everybody heads back over for live bands, deejays, and a righteous good time.

DEJA VU, 245 SOUTH NEW YORK AVENUE, ATLANTIC CITY, 609-348-4313, is a dance club that leaves all others in its wake. Throbbing music, laser lights, and celebrity-spotting are but a few of the attractions. Not a bad way to spend your evening, whether to celebrate your casino winnings or to forget your casino losses.

MEMORIES, 9518 AMHERST AVENUE, MARGATE, 609-823-2196, is where you want to go to dance the night away into sweet oblivion. And we're not talking about that newfangled electronic noise. What we are talking about is memories. Memories of rockin' 'round the clock, of seconding that emotion, and of taking a surfin' safari—good-time oldies are what it's all about.

VENTURA'S GREENHOUSE, 106 SOUTH BENSON AVENUE, MARGATE 609-822-0140, is where you would go to slam back a few beers while watching all the pretty people

milling about. It's located right on the beach, and the place to be while imbibing there is definitely the deck, which boasts a view of the beach. Day or night, the Greenhouse packs them in.

QUO VADIS, 4200 PACIFIC AVENUE, WILDWOOD, 609-522-4949, is the hip happenin' disco in town. It features strobe lights, and people have been known to dance themselves into a frenzy. I hear Quo Vadis also sponsors wet-T-shirt contests, if you're into that sort of thing.

THE MERION INN, 106 DECATUR STREET, CAPE MAY, 609-884-8363. The Merion Inn's bar, the oldest in Cape May, is decorated in the turn-of-the-century Victorian style of much of Cape May itself. Walking in, you feel as if you could be Gatsby, awaiting the imminent arrival of the lovely Daisy Buchanan. (Note to all English Lit majors: I know that Queen Victoria died decades before Gatsby met Daisy, but it's a place he'd feel comfortable in.) Feel free to order what you like, but really folks, a shot and a beer are not the libations you should be thinking of. Think martini. Think brandy. Think Gatsby. Almost forgot—the Merion has a great lunch and dinner menu, and, not surprisingly, not a hamburger in sight.

Shore drinks don't always come in mugs.

CHAPTER IV

ATLANTIC CITY

Once considered the crown jewel of the Shore, Atlantic City now exists primarily to take your crown jewels. It's no surprise to anyone that gambling is the bread and butter of this Shore town, and we're not talking about trying to win a carton of cigarettes on the big wheel. Atlantic City and Las Vegas were the only gambling centers in the United States up until a couple of years ago. Then seemingly every town with a riverboat decided to open up shop. As a result, Atlantic City had to stop resting on its collective blackjack tables and start offering some good family-style entertainment to try to lure in us suckers, er, tourists. It's been a bit of an uphill battle, but a visit to Atlantic City today shows off a cleaner, gentler place than it was ten years ago.

A Little History

The town of Atlantic City came into being in 1793 as the first settlement on Absecon Island. About fifty years later, a group of businessmen (none of whom was related to Donald Trump) came up with the idea of turning the town into a health resort. Soon people from Philadelphia and Camden hopped the rails and began the first wave of tourism into Atlantic City. By 1870, the Boardwalk (the first of its kind) was completed and soon afterward amusements were added. By the swinging 1920s, the town was a

Ripley's Believe It or Not! is devoted to the strange and wonderful.

haven for the jet set, with grand hotels built along the seashore and many diversions to be had. Broadway shows that hadn't made it to Broadway yet played there, and in 1921 some genius-minded people came up with the Miss America pageant, which kept people in town through September. Atlantic City suffered with the rest of America during the Depression and World War II, but, unlike much of America, Atlantic City didn't bounce back; after the war it did not return to its previous prominence as a vacation spot. The rich and famous boarded jets and headed off to newer, more luxurious sites around the globe. The town was quickly falling into disrepair, and the slide continued until 1978 and the dawn of casino gambling in New Jersey. The fanfare that surrounded this is hard to explain today, but back then if you wanted to gamble recreationally in America you went to Nevada or nowhere. Today, there is gambling all over the country, but Atlantic City remains the number one spot for gambling in America. In fact, Atlantic City is the number one tourist destination in the country, with some 37 million people passing through each year. Figuring that the majority of that number spend some time gambling, the average loss per person is about $1,100. Consider yourself a winner if you come in below that figure.

Things to Do

Had enough gambling for the day? Then it's time to take a stroll down the Boardwalk. A fun place to spend an hour is at **RIPLEY'S BELIEVE IT OR NOT!**, a museum dedicated to the strange and wonderful. LOCATED AT THE END OF NEW YORK AVENUE ON THE BOARDWALK (609-347-2001), the museum is a self-guided tour through such things as a life-size replica of Robert Waldow, the tallest man ever, who stood at a mind-blowing eight feet eleven inches. Or perhaps matchsticks are your bag. You won't be disappointed by the replica of the Sydney Harbor Bridge, built by Mr. Len Hughes using 160,000 matchsticks. That and so much more can be found at Ripley's, including real letters written to Mr. Ripley.

After you're done there, take a walk over to the **STEEL PIER,** located behind the Taj Mahal. With more than twenty-five rides, including the new stomach-churning Orbiter, the Steel Pier is a great place to blow off some gambling steam.

Then check out the **ATLANTIC CITY HISTORICAL MUSEUM,** THE GARDEN PIER, CONNECTICUT AVENUE AND THE BOARDWALK (609-347-5839). Featuring displays showing Atlantic City as it used to be, it's a reminder that sometimes the past, although shown in black and white, can be more colorful than the present. Speaking of color and black and white, the **ATLANTIC CITY ART CENTER** (609-347-5837) is also located on the historic Garden Pier. Its three galleries display a variety of artwork, and admission is free.

No reference to the Atlantic City of the past would be complete without mention of the rolling chairs. Simply put, you hop into a chair on wheels and get pushed to your destination along the Boardwalk. It's not a cheap thrill—a fifteen-block trip costs ten dollars—but it's interesting. Besides, the chairs and their operators are a part of the old-time Atlantic City that has pretty much disappeared elsewhere, and the fare is a welcome source of income to the chair-pushers.

Atlantic City's famous rolling chairs still glide along the Boardwalk.

Six Popular Casino Games

Most people who come to Atlantic City do so in order to gamble. That said, most people who come to Atlantic City leave with less money than they had when they got there. Gamblers lose money both because of what's known as the "house advantage" and because of a specific mindset: If you think "I can lose X amount of dollars," you'll probably lose X amount, and a few Y's for good measure. Unless you're a professional gambler, the best mindset to have is "I'm here to have some fun." Not that you shouldn't set limits for yourself—that's very important. But there's nothing wrong with walking away from a table with a tidy sum in your pocket. Here are descriptions of six of the most popular games. This should not be taken in any way as a definitive guide to gambling; consider it no more than friendly advice. Some of the offerings are strictly games of chance, while others involve some skill. Whatever you play, it will be a good idea to request a gaming guide at the casino. That will give you a highly detailed description of which games are offered.

SLOTS Known as one-armed bandits, these ubiquitous machines are a mainstay at every casino. There is no skill involved in playing them, so everybody can enjoy the thrill of hoping to see three 7s come across the screen and watch as enough quarters come pouring out to do laundry for a lifetime. The average slot machine generally pays out anywhere from ninety to ninety-nine cents on each dollar you put in. If you're intent on trying to break the bank, you should stick with machines that have a progressive jackpot. And always put in the maximum amount of coins allowed, lest you hit the big one, only to miss out on it because you put in three quarters instead of four.

BACCARAT A famously popular European game, baccarat has not taken American gamblers by storm, which is a shame, because the game offers some of the best odds in the house. The rules are somewhat complicated, but the gist of it is this: The banker (dealer) deals cards to himself and to the player (one player playing cards per table, though anyone can bet). And what you are betting on exactly is who will win, the banker or the player, or a tie. The rules of the game are set. Each participant receives two cards, and based on those, each can receive a third. Confused? Yeah, I know. But even if you don't know what's going on, betting the banker is one of the best bets in Atlantic City.

CRAPS This is where the exciting action is: people screaming, hollering, carrying on. The thrill of being part of a lucky run in craps is the most exciting thing that can happen to you in Atlantic City. Again, the rules are plentiful and complicated, but some of the best bets in the casino are made here. There are four kinds of bets, as a matter of fact. For simplicity's sake, I'll discuss the pass line bet. If you make a pass line bet, the following can happen: The roller picks up the two dice and rolls a 7 or 11, in which case you win. Or the roller rolls a 2, 3, or 12 (craps), in which case you lose. That's it. If the roller rolls a 4, 5, 6, 8, 9, or 10, then he or she continues to roll until that number is rolled again (you win), or a 7 is rolled (you lose). The other three "good" bets are the come bet, the don't pass bet, and the don't come bet. They are all variations on the pass line bet and offer roughly the same odds.

ROULETTE Many people have claimed to have a system to beat the house at roulette. They're wrong. In fact, roulette is one of the worst games to play if you intend to win systematically. But it sure is fun. There are two types of bets, known as "inside" and "outside." Inside bets are when you bet on a certain number to come up on the wheel. Say you pick 32, and 32 comes up. You win, and at 35-to-1 odds, you win a lot of money. Of course, there are 38 places for the ball to fall on the wheel (1 to 36, plus 0 and 00), so you can plainly see that 35 to 1 isn't exactly fair. The other bet, the outside bet, is when you bet on red/black, even/odd, or within a numbered range. These bets pay even money or 2 to 1, depending on the bet.

BLACKJACK Blackjack players are an interesting bunch. If you happen to sit down with serious players, you'd better know the "rules" for when to hit or stick, because they won't be afraid to show their displeasure. The beauty of casino blackjack is that an experienced player who plays the probabilities can cut the house edge to almost nil. With a good (lucky) run, a blackjack player can quickly increase his or her bankroll.

The basic strategy for blackjack is as follows: If you have between 12 and 16 and the dealer has a 7 or higher, draw. If you have between 12 and 16 and the dealer has a 2 through 6, stand. If you have 17 or higher, stay.

Blackjack offers players the ability to "double down," meaning that they can double their bets. Most casinos only allow you to draw one card. The basic strategy for this

Many people have claimed to have a system to beat the house at roulette. They're wrong.

play is: If you have an 11, double down if the dealer has a 10 or less. If you have a 10, double down if the dealer has a 9 or less. If you have a 9, double down if the dealer has a 4, 5, or 6.

You can also split pairs. The strategy is: Always split aces and 8s. Never split 4s, 5s, or 10s. Split 2s and 3s when the dealer's upcard is between 4 and 7. Split 6s when the dealer's upcard is between 3 and 6. Split 7s when the dealer's upcard is between 2 and 7. Split 9s when the dealer's upcard is between 2 and 9.

The ancient Roman decor at Ceasars is part of the experience.

POKER Relatively new to Atlantic City, poker is offered at Bally's, Caesars, Harrah's, the Sands, the Tropicana, and the Taj Mahal. Many variations are played, from five-card draw to Texas hold 'em. If you don't know what I'm talking about already, then don't bother reading on. If you do know what I'm talking about, and fancy yourself King of the Tuesday Night Game at Ed's, well, the only word I can offer you is "Caution." You don't know who you're up against.

The Hotels

This list is alphabetical, nothing more. No odds, no system, no magic.

ATLANTIC CITY HILTON CASINO HOTEL,
BOSTON AND PACIFIC AVENUES, 800-257-8677. Formerly Bally's Grand, the Atlantic City Hilton is the southernmost casino in all of gambling land. For foodies, the Oaks, featuring meat and seafood, and Peregrines', with its upscale menu and its upscale furnishings, are the two top spots.

BALLY'S PARK PLACE—A HILTON CASINO
RESORT, PARK PLACE AND THE BOARDWALK, 800-225-5977. Bally's is growing, thanks in large part to the new Wild Wild West Casino area of the hotel. Drawing a younger crowd than the main gaming section does, the Wild Wild West section offers a distinct 1800s California gold rush feel. There's a buffet restaurant called Virginia City Buffet within the Western section, but perhaps the best place for eats is Pickles, a New York–style delicatessen with sandwiches so big it's nearly

impossible to wrap your mouth around them. Pastrami tastes great with blackjack.

CAESARS ATLANTIC CITY HOTEL CASINO,

ARKANSAS AND PACIFIC AVENUES, 800-443-0104. With the ancient Roman decor, you'd half expect your water to come from aqueducts. Well, that's not the case, but Caesars does have an eighteen-foot-tall, nine-ton replica of Michelangelo's David in all his glory, and the Bacchanal, a restaurant in which you will be plied with almost obscene amounts of food and drink until your toga is bursting at the seams. Caesars is also the site of the decidedly un-Roman Planet Hollywood restaurant.

CLARIDGE CASINO HOTEL, INDIANA AVENUE AT

BRIGHTON PARK, 800-257-8585. One of the more inexpensive stays in Atlantic City can be had at the Claridge, a smallish hotel in the center of town. The structure was built in 1930 to look like the Empire State Building, minus a hundred or so floors. The casino area is notoriously cramped, so it's not much fun to walk around watching the gamblers gamble. However, the Claridge does offer more lower-stakes tables than any other casino in town. As far as food goes, it's Fun Central. Eating at the Twenties allows you to get in touch with your inner flapper as you dine on Lindbergh's Lobster Tails. For a quick bite, check out Wok & Roll, a Chinese fast-food restaurant that gets my vote for coolest name.

HARRAH'S CASINO HOTEL, 1725 BRIGANTINE

BOULEVARD, 800-242-7724. Away from the hustle and bustle of the Boardwalk, Harrah's opened up its doors in 1980 in the hope of drawing people to what was then the only hotel on the other side of town. It did draw them, and today the glass-enclosed Harrah's tower is one of the town's biggest attractions. Located on the bay, there is a marina so you can dock and gamble. When you sea lovers get the urge to eat, the William Fisk Seafood Co. is the place to go for just-caught-twenty-minutes-ago fresh seafood, cooked to order any way you like it. If you want seafood but want to enjoy it in that famous buffet-style setting, check out the Fantasea Reef Buffet, with loads of crab legs, shrimp, and the like waiting to be devoured.

RESORTS CASINO HOTEL, NORTH CAROLINA

AVENUE AND THE BOARDWALK, 800-336-6378. This used to be Merv Griffin's place. When it opened on May 26,

Caesars is also the site of Planet Hollywood.

1978, it was the first casino in Atlantic City. Its eight restaurants are anchored by Capriccio, an authentic Italian restaurant overlooking the Atlantic, and Ginza, a Japanese restaurant that serves up the freshest sushi imaginable in a traditional Japanese-style setting.

SANDS HOTEL AND CASINO, INDIANA AVENUE AND BRIGHTON PARK, 800-257-8580. The Sands Hotel may be the most often referred-to casino hotel in town if for no other reason than that it's Atlantic City's prime arena for boxing, which makes it known the world over. From the outside, the Sands resembles nothing more than a giant gleaming black box. Its China Moon restaurant specializes in authentic Cantonese dishes. The Sands' Epic Buffet may be the best in town. With epic amounts of Italian, American, and Asian cuisine served amid epic amounts of memorabilia from epic movies, the word "epic" may lose all meaning after you enjoy an epic meal.

Casinos are bustling around the clock.

SHOWBOAT CASINO HOTEL, DELAWARE AVENUE AND THE BOARDWALK, 800-621-0200. The Showboat, as its name suggests, has a New Orleans theme. Dixieland jazz is both piped in and played by real musicians as you walk around. For a Dixieland meal, stop in at the Mississippi Steak and Seafood Co.

TROPICANA CASINO AND RESORT, IOWA AVENUE AND THE BOARDWALK, 800-257-6227. The Tropicana is perhaps the most family-friendly casino on the strip. One great attraction is the ride to the Top of the Trop in a glass-enclosed elevator. Once at the top, you get the kind of panoramic views of Atlantic City that only the high rollers were once privy to. The family-friendly atmosphere suffers a bit when you encounter Hooters, a theme restaurant serving up your basic American fare, with scenery provided by the waitstaff wearing tight orange shorts. For more refined tastes, there's always Il Verdi, featuring Northern Italian delicacies.

TRUMP PLAZA HOTEL AND CASINO, MISSISSIPPI AVENUE AND THE BOARDWALK, 800-677-7378. Perhaps the classiest of Atlantic City casinos (if that's not an oxymoron). No expense was spared when this place was built in 1984. The views from the rooms are splendid. The Trump Plaza is connected to the Atlantic City Convention Center, and rooms here are in high demand whenever Miss America comes to town. On the food front, Ivanka's, named after Mr. Trump's oldest daughter, features some of the finest dining in town, and Max's Steak House serves up fine food in an old-time New York gentleman's club atmosphere.

TRUMP MARINA CASINO RESORT, HURON AVENUE AND BRIGANTINE BOULEVARD, 800-365-8786. The other hotel on the bay side, the Trump Marina competes with Harrah's for your bay-side gambling dollar. The Marina has a definite Los Angeles/Miami feel, and the restaurants certainly match the mood. The Deck is an outdoor affair with a basic American menu. Since it's outdoors, it's only open seasonally. There is also the Upstairs Grille, which has California cuisine served both traditionally and Wolfgang Puckish.

TRUMP TAJ MAHAL CASINO RESORT,
1000 BOARDWALK, 800-825-8786. The Taj, as it's affectionately known, is quite possibly the single gaudiest place in all of New Jersey, and that includes my Aunt Jo's living room. When you arrive, you're greeted by nine imposing pachyderms guarding the entrance, and, once inside, you'll gawk at the more than $14 million worth of crystal chandeliers hanging from what seems to be every square inch of ceiling. When it was built, it laid claim to being the biggest casino in the world, but now the MGM Grand in Las Vegas has that title. Nonetheless, it would take a Rockefeller not to be impressed with the opulence of Atlantic City's centerpiece structure. As far as dining goes, there is the Scheherazade, which overlooks the baccarat pit and features international dishes. Dynasty has a sushi bar and virtually any type of Asian cuisine you can shake a chopstick at.

TRUMP WORLD'S FAIR CASINO HOTEL AT TRUMP PLAZA, FLORIDA AVENUE AND THE BOARDWALK, 800-677-7378. Housed in what used to be the Playboy Hotel and Casino, this is Trump's "little" casino. Not nearly as fancy as the others, it surely will be one day, if past Trump development is anything to go by. The best place to eat at the World's Fair is O'Flynn's Irish Pub, where you can enjoy typical pub food while quaffing some beer.

CHAPTER V

EVERYTHING ELSE UNDER THE SUN

You've sat on the beach. You've swum in the ocean. You've eaten enough food to last until Christmas. You've shopped, you've gambled, you've climbed Barnegat Light.

Now what?

Well, for starters, I never told you some of my Shore travel shortcuts, or suggested how to go about finding a place to stay once you are at the Shore. You know. The basics.

And a reminder: Before you leave the Shore, be sure to pick up a souvenir or two.

Getting There

I can't wait until NASA or some such group perfects the molecular transfer of human beings. Step into the contraption, punch in your destination, and presto! you're transported to anywhere you want to go, including the Jersey Shore, especially at five o'clock on Friday afternoon in summer. Anything to avoid Parkway traffic, although I'd imagine if everyone were using the transporter at once you'd wind up missing some luggage. A small price to pay, if you ask me.

Traffic in New Jersey is a way of life, and trying to get to the Shore is not exempt from this horrific fact. Herewith are some tips that may help you along your route.

IF YOU'RE COMING FROM THE NORTH

If you're coming from the north, yours is but one of the half million cars that will be jockeying for position on the southbound Garden State Parkway on any given summer weekend. Unfortunately, there's really no avoiding it. Traffic gets especially backed up from the Essex tolls down to the Union tolls, and really picks up steam when you get to the Governor Alfred E. Driscoll Bridge, which takes you over the Raritan River. The reason this happens is that no fewer than seven highways–the Parkway, the Turnpike, Routes 1, 9, 35, and 440, and I-287–all meet within a three-mile radius around those parts. If you travel the Parkway, there's really no avoiding this tie-up, but if you're coming from I-287 or 440, you can hop on Route 35, take the Victory Bridge, and catch up with the Parkway five miles down the road.

When you're traveling through Monmouth County, Route 34 might be a better bet than the Parkway. Despite such inconveniences as traffic lights, the road is definitely less traveled.

IF YOU'RE COMING FROM THE WEST

For starters, if you're destination is Long Beach Island, take Route 70 to Route 72. It takes you through the Pinelands and right to the bridge to the island, where you're bound to sit in some traffic.

If you're headed to Atlantic City, you can forgo the Atlantic City Expressway in favor of the Black Horse Pike. While it's slower, it's certainly more scenic and relatively stress free, exactly what you need when you're headed to Atlantic City.

WHEN YOU'RE THERE In Ocean and Atlantic Counties, Ocean Drive is the preferred route for many reasons. First, there's usually less traffic than on the alternatives, the Parkway or Route 9. But more important, it offers views of

You don't need a passport to get to the Jersey Shore from inland, but do plan ahead.

the Shore that you can't get anywhere else. With the Atlantic on one side and the Intracoastal Waterway on the other, you'll be awestruck by the sights and smells you'll encounter.

COMING AND GOING Especially on weekends, do everything in your power to arrive before 5 PM or after 9 PM, which means leaving your Bergen County home before 3 PM or after 7 PM. You'll miss most of the traffic. Leaving northern New Jersey at three in the afternoon should get you there with minimal traffic. The weather is the most important factor when you leave the Shore on Sunday. If it's cloudy, wet, or cold, everyone will be trying to escape early. So don't. Conversely, on a beautiful day, people tend to extend their vacations as long as possible, which means they're not leaving until late afternoon. Unless you don't mind sitting in continuous traffic, I encourage you to skedaddle by 3 PM at the latest.

🍥 🍥 🍥

Finding a Place to Stay

For some of us, finding a place to stay at the Shore is as easy as paying a mortgage (or having parents who finished paying the mortgage years ago). You know who you are, and you needn't bother with this section. For others, perhaps you're even luckier: you don't own your own place, but your aunt has said that you can come down anytime you want. That's easy too, but don't forget to clean up after yourself, or that same aunt will quickly be revoking all privileges.

What if you don't have your own place and you don't know anybody who is willing to put you and your family up for the week. You have to make some decisions. Do you want to rent a home? Stay in a motel or hotel? A bed-and-breakfast or guest house, perhaps? There are many options.

If you're considering a house rental, keep several things in mind. For starters, there's the cost. Oceanside homes are generally two to three times more expensive than those on the bay side. If you do want an oceanfront house, it's important to make that decision early—many of the best homes are snatched up by January. Some things to ask your rental agent are how much of a security deposit is required, whether you need renter's insurance, and whether pets are allowed. It's also important to find out what amenities are included. Is there air-conditioning? How well equipped is the kitchen? Is there a microwave?

Rule one if you're planning a stay at the Shore: Plan ahead. Then again, it's close enough to home for a spontaneous day trip.

Renting a house with a group of friends or extended family is a great way to spend a vacation to share both experiences and costs, and there will never be a lack of things to do. That is, of course, if you like the people you're with.

As far as hotels and motels go, cost is an obvious factor, but not the only thing to go by. Whereas inexpensive motels can be found in more touristy towns, such as Wildwood and Seaside Heights, a stay at a fancier hotel in Bay Head or Longport can run into hundreds of dollars per night. If you really prefer the style of one place over another, it may be worth it to you to shorten your stay by a night or two to make up for the greater expense of a a quieter town or more elaborate lodging. Many of the same questions you might ask when renting a home are applicable to finding a motel or hotel. Some rooms offer efficiency kitchens and sitting rooms, while others have more Motel 6 chic: two beds, a television, and a small bathroom. Just as nicer houses get rented early, rooms at the better hotels get booked early. The earlier you make a decision, the more choices you'll have.

Bed-and-breakfasts and guest houses sometimes offer the best of both worlds (though not always). Balance the possible lack of TV, private bath, and in-room phones against the charm of curlicued carved furniture, lace curtains, and wallpaper that looks like a flower-covered trellis. Looking at the bright side of the B and B/guest house continuum, think of a place that's quaint and homey but where you don't have to make your own bed. The prices are generally higher than at motels and hotels, but you do get more for your money, including (usually) beach badges, beach towels, breakfast, and sometimes even the use of bicycles. You should certainly make reservations at least a month in advance, but, as always, the earlier the better. Well-known places or establishments that have recently been favorably reviewed in travel publications are likely to fill up even earlier, of course. And if you continue to come back year after year to the same place, expect to get your choice of rooms and perhaps even a discount.

The organizations listed on the next page may be helpful in your search for places to stay at the Shore (and everywhere else in the state, for that matter).

Bed-and-breakfast or sea-view motel—whichever you prefer, call ahead if you want to stay the night.

Ten Great Cape May
Bed-and-Breakfasts/Guest Houses

Why not Bay Head? Isn't there any place to stay at
Loveladies so that I can pretend to myself during my
morning walk that I own one of those great geometric
beachfront houses? Didn't the author of this book ever
hear of golf resorts like the Seaview Marriott? Those are
all good questions, and the sources listed in the margin
may very well be able to help you get the answers you're
looking for. Why, then, single out Cape May for a listing
of places to stay? Because, among all the towns along the
Shore, it's the one most closely identified with just this
type of lodging. It's carved a place for itself in regional if
not national vacation lore. It's just one of those places you
go when you want to stay at a great bed-and-breakfast.
The ones I've listed here are some that particularly
appealed to me.

CAPTAIN MEY'S INN, 202 OCEAN STREET, 800-981-
3702, is named for the founder of Cape May, Captain
Cornelius J. Mey, who came to these shores in 1621 work-
ing for the Dutch West India Company. The inn that bears
his name has eight rooms, including one with a Jacuzzi; all
the rooms have private baths. Breakfast includes the usual
treats, such as French toast, homemade breads, crepes, and
eggs Benedict, with a soothing background of classical
music. The inn is open year-round, and there's a wrap-
around porch and a landscaped courtyard. Summer room
rates approach $200, with much lower rates off-season.

THE CLIVEDEN INN, 709 COLUMBIA AVENUE, 800-
884-2420, is in the heart of the Historic District, and conveniently located two blocks from the beach. All the
rooms have private baths and air-conditioning. Rates are
from $100 to $150 per night.

COLUMNS BY THE SEA, 1513 BEACH DRIVE, 609-
884-2228, was built in 1910 by a Philadelphia physician.
There was no architect present at any point during the
design proceedings, and the whole thing was built accord-
ing to the whims of the doctor, with the result that the
whole place is something of a curiosity. There are twenty
large rooms in the mansion, with windows all over. It's
located away from the bustling center of town, which
makes it a perfect place for absolutely quiet relaxation.
Rates are from $150 to $260 per night.

5
Helpful
Organizations

**AUTOMOBILE
ASSOCIATION OF
AMERICA**
973-377-7200

**NEW JERSEY BED
AND BREAKFAST
ASSOCIATION**
800-992-2632

**NEW JERSEY
HOTEL-MOTEL
ASSOCIATION**
609-586-9000

**NEW JERSEY
DIVISION OF TRAVEL
AND TOURISM**
609-292-2470 OR
800-JERSEY-7

**OCEAN COUNTY
TOURISM
INFORMATION LINE**
800-ENJOY-33

THE DUKE OF WINDSOR, 817 WASHINGTON
STREET, 609-884-1355 OR 800-826-8973, stands out for
many reasons, including the forty-five-foot tower that
houses two of the guest rooms. The Queen Anne–style
building boasts stained-glass windows and a dining room
with an elaborate plaster ceiling. Most rooms have a private shower or bath; room rates vary depending on bath
facilities as well as season.

THE HENRY SAWYER INN, 732 COLUMBIA AVENUE,
800-449-5667, was built in 1877 by the then-treasurer of
Cape May. He'd be proud to know that the money is still
rolling in. The Henry Sawyer offers packages throughout the
year, with such amenities as roses, chocolates, dinner certifi-
cates, and more. Rates for the packages vary widely,
depending on how long you stay and what package you
choose. Nonpackage nightly rates are from $85 to $185.

**Some inns give
you chocolate
on your pillow—
though not
quite this many,
and probably
not in a heart-
shaped box.**

PHARO'S, 617 COLUMBIA AVENUE, 609-884-9380, has
been standing since 1867. Obviously things in the outside
world have changed significantly since then. As a result,
Pharo's has a television in the common sitting room for a
"small touch of reality." Rates are $110 to $150 per night.

PLUM PALACE, 1002 WASHINGTON STREET, 609-884-
8406, overlooks the city park, complete with a fish pond,
barbecues, a playground, and fourteen clay tennis courts.
"Well-behaved children are always welcome," the Plum
Palace says in its brochure. Rates are from $95 to $195
per night.

POOR RICHARD'S INN, AT 17 JACKSON STREET, 609-
884-3536, has its own listing on the National Register of
Historic Places, but, curiously, has opted for more modern
touches than many other inns in town. The innkeepers tell
you right off the bat that they're not aiming for total
Victorian authenticity, but rather to make you feel at
home. The rates are reasonable, ranging from $45 to $139,
depending on the season and on whether you want a private or shared bath.

THE SUMMER COTTAGE INN, 613 COLUMBIA AVENUE, 609-884-4948, was commissioned to be built in 1867 as a family summer vacation cottage, and it remained so until the early 1900s, when it became a guest house. All the rooms are decorated with the expected Victorian touch and have private baths, and there's a porch complete with plants and a wicker swing. The Italianate inn's cupola is lit at night. Rates range from from $85 to $175 per night, depending upon the season and the specific room.

WHITE DOVE COTTAGE, 619 HUGHES STREET, 609-884-0613, has two suites and four rooms, each with its own personality—and its own name: Lady Kathy and Lady Susann are the suites, and Princess Jillian, Countess Karen, Sir Paul, and Lord Jason are the rooms. A special feature that may take place any time from January through March is the Weekend Inn Mystery: You can be "the sleuth, suspect, victim, or murderer." Rates for all rooms run from $80 to $215 per night.

ROUGHING IT At the other end of the spectrum from the architectural and culinary gingerbread of Cape May are campgrounds, areas both public and private where afternoon tea means a bottle of Snapple, dinner means foil-wrapped pocket stew, and the running water may flow from an outdoor faucet. Here's a very short list (for information purposes, not personal recommendation) of some of the many campgrounds in the general region of the Shore.

Barnegat Bay Campground, BARNEGAT, 609-698-3344
Brookville Campground, BARNEGAT, 609-698-3134
Long Beach Island Trailer Park,
  BEACH HAVEN, 609-492-9151
Frontier Campground, OCEAN VIEW, 800-277-4109
Holly Shores, WILDWOOD, 609-886-1234
Seashore Campsites, CAPE MAY, 609-884-4010

In addition to the dozens of private campgrounds, some of which offer swimming and other recreational facilities, the state park system has a number of campsites that offer varying degrees of wilderness experience. Perhaps the best known is the very large and varied WHARTON STATE FOREST (609-561-3262 OR 609-561-0024).

Even if your inn has electricity (and of course it will), there's nothing like a candlelit dinner in a Victorian dining room.

99

Ten Souvenirs You Must Come Home With

Summer isn't over. But just in case winter comes early this year, here are some items guaranteed to help you preserve your memories of the perfect wave, the glowing sunset, the endless beach, the bustling boardwalk, and everything else that you'll want to revisit before your next real trip to the Shore.

CAPE MAY DIAMONDS Cape May Diamonds. Sound pretty special, no? Well, they're not. Sorry. They're just pure quartz crystals that wash ashore, but they sure do look good. Their size varies; most are about the size of a pebble, although some as large as eggs have been found. When you see them in their natural state on the beach, they look nothing like diamonds. In fact, they look like any old pebble or rock the size of an egg. But after they're polished, cut, and faceted, they look remarkably like real diamonds, and can be mounted in gold or silver to create quite lovely jewelry. Hey, anytime you can buy an engagement ring for $125, you know you've really found something special.

SKEEBALL TICKETS Knocking your knees against the Skeeball machine and yelping in pain notwithstanding, the game offers a chance for everyone to play. Sure, there's some skill involved, but that doesn't prevent anyone from enjoying the game. And talk about instant gratification! As you rack up the points, those tickets come popping out of the slot, encouraging you to put more money in so that you can get more tickets and eventually trade them in for...a lot of junk. Let's face it: Chances are, you'll be walking out of there with two bouncy balls and a back-scratcher. So you might as well keep a string of those tickets, throw them in a scrapbook, and leave the Spice Girls trading cards for someone else.

A PRINT OR WATERCOLOR OF A SHORESCAPE
And not a $30,000 one either. Buy the kitschiest one
you can find and hang it in your basement. There are
certain things to look for when making this purchase.
There should be no fewer than six seagulls in the scene,
at least one person somewhere, a wave crashing on
the sand, and a lighthouse in the distance. The sky can
be either blue or slate gray.

**NO FEWER THAN THREE TINS OF SALTWATER
TAFFY** Although originally an Atlantic City delicacy, saltwater taffy has spread up and down New Jersey's coast like butter
on a hot bagel. It's sweeter than pure cane sugar, comes in
wildly various colors and flavors, valiantly attempts to pull out
any fillings you may have, and is best served at room tempera-
ture. A cautionary note, however. Saltwater taffy contains
absolutely no saltwater.

SEASHELLS FROM THE SEASHORE A wonderful
morning tradition is the family walk along the beach with
everyone searching for the most beauteous of seashells.
Everyone takes part in this time-honored tradition. Once
you get home, however, there seems to be little use for
three pounds of the stuff. What to do? The answer is this:
Buy one of those glass bowls that look like a giant brandy
snifter, and pile the shells up in there, with the bigger ones
at the top. Display on a table, probably in the vicinity of
the watercolor you bought.

**Bring home a
painted
shorescape as a
souvenir—or
paint your own.**

**A BIG PUFFY SWEATSHIRT WITH THE NAME
OF THE TOWN YOU WERE IN** Everybody loves
sweatshirts. Especially big puffy ones. Everyone also loves
the beach. Ergo, buying a big puffy sweatshirt with a
Shore town's name emblazoned on it seems like a good
idea. Imagine yourself on a Sunday morning in January.
The thermometer reads seven degrees, there's been snow
on the ground for two weeks, and you are feeling like a
frozen piece of leftover meatloaf. You're getting dressed,
and you spot that sweatshirt you bought last summer. You
put it on, and you're transported back to sunny days and
warm temperatures. You dance a happy dance and start
singing show tunes. Life couldn't be any better. Aren't you
glad you bought that sweatshirt?

**Postcards:
The last
vestige
of good taste
in America.**

POSTCARDS Postcards are the last vestige of good taste in America. There's enough space to write what needs to be said and nothing else, and some of them are downright handsome. There's the ubiquitous "Greetings from..." series, the ones that show towns the way they used to look, the ones with cheese-cake shots of models in skimpy beachwear. Ah yes, the last vestige of good taste in America: the postcard.

YOUR BEACH BADGE Although a beach badge doesn't carry the same cachet as ski-lift tickets on your jacket zipper, saving your beach badges is just the proper thing to do. Put them on your backpack, and you're sure to be the center of conversation.

A GIANT STUFFED ANIMAL Take twenty dollars. Throw said twenty dollars to the wind in an attempt to beat the boardwalk gods of chance and win a twelve-foot stuffed giraffe. Repeat until you win. Then carry your winnings around to show people that it can be done. Once you have your twelve-foot giraffe safely back in your suburban digs, display it as a testament to your hard work and dedication.

EMPTY PLASTIC COIN CONTAINERS FROM ATLANTIC CITY You may walk out of Atlantic City with nothing but lint in your pockets, but be sure to take as many of those giant plastic cups that you can get your hands on. They serve many purposes; they can be anything from your own personal change holder to a great drinking glass for your next block party. A must-have.

PHOTOGRAPHY CREDITS

New Jersey Monthly Press wishes to thank the organizations and individuals whose illustrations are used in this book.

Courtesy of the Atlantic City Convention and Visitors Authority, pages 83, 84, 86, 89, 90

Courtesy of Tom Briglia for the Wildwoods, pages 18,19,44

Courtesy of Caesars Atlantic City, page 88

Courtesy of Cape May Department of Tourism, pages 30, 31, 53

Courtesy of Walter Choroszewski, pages 17, 21, 29, 32, 38, 42, 96

Courtesy of Jenkinson's Boardwalk, page 50

Courtesy of Johnson's Popcorn, page 24

Courtesy of the New Jersey Commerce and Economic Growth Commission, 34

Courtesy of the Ocean County Department of Public Affairs, 13, 47

Map, page 8, by Yong-Hun Chon

Asbury Park, 36

Atlantic City, 53, 73, 74, 75, 76, 83–91
   History, 53, 84, 85
   Things to do, 85
   Casino games, 86–88
   Hotels, 88–91

Atlantic County entries
   Atlantic City, 83–91
   Longport, 38
   Margate City, 32, 52

Avalon, 28, 59, 63

Avon-by-the-Sea, 37

Barnegat Light, 38, 45. 5—51, 52

Barnegat Light State Park, 52

Bars, 78–80
   Bar Anticipation, 78
   Club X S, 78
   D'Jai's, 78
   Deja Vu, 79
   Ej's, 79
   Hudson House Bar, 79
   Jason's, 78
   Martell's Sea Breeze, 78
   Memories, 79
   Merion Inn, 80
   Osprey Hotel, 31, 78
   Quo Vadis, 80
   Sea Shell Motel and Club, 79
   Ventura's Greenhouse, 79
   Yakety Yak Café, 79

Bay Head, 25–26, 59, 68

Beaches, 16, 17, 18, 19, 20, 22, 24, 25, 26–27, 28, 29, 31, 32, 33–34, 35

Beach Haven, 16–17, 43, 45, 46, 50, 52, 54, 57, 60, 61, 64, 66, 67, 68, 69, 70, 72, 73, 76
   Fantasy Island Amusement Park, 16, 43
   Southern Ocean County Chamber of Commerce, 17
   Surflight Theatre, 16, 54–55
   Veterans Bicentennial Park, 17

Belmar, 15–16, 42, 45, 48, 57, 66, 70, 75
   Belmar Five Mile Run, 16
   Belmar Marina, 15, 16, 45
   Belmar Playland, 42

Huisman Gazebo, 15
Miracle Mile, 16
Payanoe Plaza Concert Series, 15, 16
Taylor Pavilion, 15, 16
Walking tour, 15

Bicycle riding, 17, 22, 49
Island Beach State Park, 49
Ocean City Boardwalk, 23–24, 49
Sandy Hook, 49

Boardwalks and boardwalk
amusement parks, 16, 17, 18, 21, 23–24,
27, 30, 42–44, 49
Belmar Playland, 42
Casino Pier, 42
Dinosaur Beach Adventure
Theme Park, 44
Fantasy Island, 43
Funtown Amusement Pier, 42
Jenkinson's, 21, 50
Lucky Leo's Arcade, 42
Morey's Pier and Theme Parks, 44
Park Place, 43–44
Playland's Castaway Cove, 43
Point Pleasant Boardwalk, 21, 42
Sand Trap Miniature Golf, 43
Seaside Heights Boardwalk, 42–43
Settler's Mill Miniature Golf, 43
Water Works, 43

Bradley Beach, 24–25, 68, 70, 75
Victorian Gazebo, 24
Miniature golf, 25

Breakfast, 64–65
Bagel Bank, 65
Bagels and Beyond, 64
Brian's Waffle House and
Family Restaurant, 65
Captain John's Mr. Breakfast, 64
Chicken and the Egg, 64–65
Mad Batter, 65
Mallon's, 65
Rusty Rudder, 65
Wally Mitchell's, 64

Brigantine, 55

Candy, snacks, 73–75
Chippy's, 73

Country Kettle Fudge, 73
Fralinger's Original Salt Water Taffy, 74
Hankins' Candies, 74
James' Original Salt Water Taffy, 75
Johnson's Popcorn, 74
Rauhauser's Own Make Candies, 74
Shriver's Salt Water
Taffy and Fudge, 74
Steak King and Pizza, 74
Stutz Candies, 73

Cape May, 30–31, 47, 53, 56, 65, 67, 97–99
Cape May diamonds, 31
Inns, 97–99
Mid-Atlantic Center for the Arts, 30
Sunset Beach, 31
Washington Street Mall, 30

Cape May County entries
Avalon, 28
Cape May City, 30–1
Ocean City, 23–24
Sea Isle City, 19–20
Stone Harbor, 28
Wildwood, 18–19

Children's activities, 20, 21, 50–51
Area 54, 51
Bayview Avenue beach, 50
Bayview Park, 50
Jenkinson's Aquarium, 21, 50
Jenkinson's Beach, 21, 50
Just Bead It, 50
Market Days (Ocean City), 23, 51
Ocean City Aquarium, 51
Play by the Bay, 20

Cultural activities, 54–55
Great Auditorium
(Ocean Grove), 29, 54
Boardwalk Pavilion
(Ocean Grove), 29, 54
Historic Cold Spring Village, 55
Long Beach Island Foundation
of the Arts and Sciences, 54
Surflight Theater, 16, 54–55
Ocean City Pops, 55

Deal, 36

Dinner, 75–77

Bayou Café, 76
Captain's Table, 77
Chef Ed's, 76
Crab's Claw, 76
Draughting Table, 75
410 Bank Street, 77
Kokomo's, 77
Moonstruck, 75
Old Mill Inn, 75
O'Neill's Bar, Grill, and
    Guest House, 76
Russo's, 77
Sindia, 76
Terrace Tavern, 76
Tony's Baltimore Grille, 76
Van Scoy's Bistro, 77

Excursion boats, 46–47
Big Blue Cruiser–Whale Watcher, 47
Black Whale III, 46
Cape May Whale Watcher, 47
River Belle, 46
Wild Goose, 46
Yankee Schooner, 47

Fireworks, 21

Fishing, 45–47

Food and drink, 63–80

Harvey Cedars, 67, 72

History and historic sites, 52–53, 85
Atlantic City Historical Museum, 53
Barnegat Lighthouse State Park, 52
Cape May Lighthouse, 53
Emlen Physick Estate, 53
Hereford Inlet Lighthouse, 53
Long Beach Island
    Historical Association, 52
Lucy the Elephant, 52–53
Ocean City Historical Museum, 52
Twin Lights Historic Site, 34

House rentals, 95–96

Ice cream and ices, 68–69
Beach Plum, 68
Café Vacio, 69
Dorcas, 68
Duffer's, 69

Hobby Horse, 69
Jake's, 69
Ralph's, 68
Show Place, 68
Sundae Times, 68
Sweet Note, 69
Tory's, 69

Island Beach State Park, 34, 49

Jenkinson's, 21, 59

Kayaks, 47–48

Lavallette, 27–28, 68, 76

Lighthouses, 34, 38, 52, 54

Lodging information, 97

Long Beach Island, 50, 52, 54

Long Branch, 35, 71
Seven Presidents Oceanfront Park, 35

Longport, 38

Loveladies, 38, 54

Lunch, 71–73
Foodies, 72
Max's Hot Dogs, 71–72
Midway Steak House, 72
Raspberry Café, 72
Saw Mill, 72
Subs and Such, 72–73
Whistle Stop, 73
White House, 73

Manasquan, 31–32, 76

Mantoloking, 37

Margate City, 32, 52
Lucy the Elephant, 32, 52

Miniature golf, 25, 43

Monmouth County entries
Asbury Park, 36
Avon-by-the-Sea, 37
Belmar, 15–16
Bradley Beach, 24–25
Deal, 36
Long Branch, 35
Manasquan, 31–32
Ocean Grove, 29–30

Sandy Hook, 33–34
Sea Bright, 35
Sea Girt, 37
Spring Lake, 26–27

Nature centers, 55–56
    Marine Mammal Stranding
        Center, 55–56
    Nature Center of Cape May, 56
    Wetlands Institute, 56

North Wildwood, 53

Ocean City, 23–24, 43, 46, 49, 51, 54, 65,
    67, 69, 73, 76
    Music Pier, 23, 54
    Gillian's Wonderland Pier, 24

Ocean County entries
    Barnegat Light, 38
    Bay Head, 25–26
    Beach Haven, 16–17
    Island Beach State Park, 34
    Lavallette, 27–28
    Loveladies, 37
    Mantoloking, 37
    Point Pleasant Beach, 21–22
    Seaside Heights, 17–18
    Seaside Park, 37
    Ship Bottom, 39
    Surf City, 22

Ocean Grove, 29–30, 54, 58, 72, 75
    Boardwalk Pavilion, 29, 54
    Great Auditorium, 29, 54
    Tent City, 29

Parasailing, 48

Pizza, 70–71
    Famous Lou Michaels, 70
    Joey Tomatoes, 70

Mack and Manco's, 71
Maruca's, 71
Mike's, 70
Mr. D's, 71
Panzone's, 70
Vic's, 70–71

Playgrounds, 20, 50

Point Pleasant Beach,
    21–22, 42, 45, 46, 50, 58, 73
    Jenkinson's, 21, 22, 50
    Risden's, 22

Sandy Hook, 33–34, 49
    Fort Hancock, 33–34
    Gunnison Beach
        (clothing optional beach), 34
    Twin Lights Historic Site, 34

Sea Bright, 35

Seafood, 66–67
    Beach Haven Fishery, 66
    Boathouse Restaurant, 67
    Bookers New England
        Seafood House, 67
    Harvey Cedars Shellfish company, 67
    Lobster House, 67
    M & M Steam Bar, 66
    Seafood Garden, 66–67
    Yellow Fin, 66
    Zelbe's, 66

Sea Girt, 37
Sea Isle City, 19–21
    Beachcomber Walks, 20
    Concerts Under the Stars, 20
    Fun City, 20
    Play by the Bay, 20
Seashells, 57

Seaside Heights, 17–18, 42–43, 72
  Casino Pier, 42

Seaside Park, 37, 71, 72

Ship Bottom, 39, 43, 48, 50, 59, 73

Shopping, 26, 28, 29, 30, 57–61
  Bookstore (Beach Haven), 60
  Christmas Island (Cape May), 61
  Custom Leather Shop
    (Ocean City), 61
  Fly Away Kites (Belmar), 57–58
  Jolly Tar ((Bay Head), 59
  Kathie's Surf City
    Smoke Shop (Surf City), 59
  Kite Store (Surf City), 59
  Mickeyland (Ocean Grove), 58
  Mod Hatter (Beach Haven), 61
  Mrs. Duff's Gift Shoppe (Surf City), 59
  Nostalgic Nonsense (Belmar), 57
  Ooh-La-La (Beach Haven), 60
  Point Pleasant Antique Emporium
    (Point Pleasant Beach), 58
  Ric's Aloha Classics (Beach Haven), 61
  Ron Jons Surf Shop (Ship Bottom), 59
  Rubber Stamp Act (Belmar), 57
  Schooner's Wharf (Beach Haven), 60
  Sea Life Gallery (Surf City), 59
  Time Machine
    (Point Pleasant Beach), 58
  Washington Street Mall
    (Cape May), 30

Somers Point, 67

Sports rentals and rides, 48
  Island Surf and Sail, 48
  Parasail, Inc., 48
  Shark River Water Sports, 48
  Silver Bullet, 48

Spring Lake, 26–27, 68, 75

Stone Harbor, 29, 56, 67, 75

Surf City, 22, 50, 59, 64, 66, 70, 73

Sushi, 67
  Engleside Sushi Bar, 67
  Harumi's Ichiban, 67
  Kuishimbo, 67
  Tokyo Palace, 67
  Umi, 67

Volleyball, 16, 22

Washington Street Mall (Cape May), 30

Whale watching, 46–47

Wildwood, 18–19, 43–44, 45, 47, 48, 65,
  67, 69, 71, 73, 74, 75
  Boardwalk Classic Car Show, 19
  International Kite Festival, 19
  Irish Fall Festival, 19
  Model Aircraft Beach Fly-in
  Mummer's Brigade, 19
  National Marbles Tournament, 19
  National Speed
    Slide Championship, 19
  New Jersey State Harley
    Owner's Group Rally, 19
  Pirates Weekend, 19
  Polka Spree-by-the-Sea, 19
  Santa Claus, 19

Wildwood Crest, 77